教材项目规划小组
Teaching Material Project Planning Group

严美华	姜明宝	王立峰
田小刚	崔邦焱	俞晓敏
赵国成	宋永波	郭　鹏

加拿大方咨询小组
Canadian Consulting Group

Dr. Robert Shanmu Chen

Mr. Zheng Zhining

University of British Columbia

Dr. Helen Wu

University of Toronto

Mr. Wang Renzhong

McGill University

中国国家汉办规划教材

Hanban

NEW PRACTICAL CHINESE READER

(2nd Edition)

3

新实用汉语课本

刘珣 主编

课 本
TEXTBOOK

英文注释
Annotated in English

编　者：张凯　刘社会　陈曦
　　　　左珊丹　施家炜　刘珣
英译审订：Jerry Schmidt　余心乐

北京语言大学出版社
BEIJING LANGUAGE AND CULTURE
UNIVERSITY PRESS

（第2版）

图书在版编目（CIP）数据

新实用汉语课本：英文注释.3 /刘珣主编.
—2版.—北京：北京语言大学出版社，2012.4（2014.9重印）
ISBN 978-7-5619-3255-1

Ⅰ.新… Ⅱ.刘… Ⅲ.汉语—对外汉语教学—教材
Ⅳ. H195.4

中国版本图书馆CIP数据核字（2012）第046661号

书　　　名：新实用汉语课本（第2版 英文注释）课本 3
中文编辑：王亚莉　付彦白
英文编辑：侯晓娟
责任印制：汪学发

出版发行：北京语言大学出版社
社　　址：北京市海淀区学院路 15 号　　邮政编码：100083
网　　址：www.blcup.com
电　　话：国内发行 8610-82303650/3591/3651
　　　　　海外发行 8610-82300309/0361/3080/3365
　　　　　编辑部 8610-82303647/3592/3395
　　　　　读者服务部 8610-82303653
　　　　　网上订购电话 8610-82303908
　　　　　客户服务信箱 service@blcup.com
印　　刷：保定市中画美凯印刷有限公司
经　　销：全国新华书店

版　　次：2012 年 4 月第 2 版　2014 年 9 月第 5 次印刷
开　　本：889毫米×1194毫米　1/16　印张：18.5
字　　数：308千字
书　　号：ISBN 978-7-5619-3255-1 /H.12034
　　　　　07000

第二十七课

Lesson 27

入乡随俗

When in Rome, do as the Romans do.

When you live in a place with a different culture, you may not be used to the local customs. The local people may also have the same feeling about your own customs. How do we deal with these cultural differences? Our main characters are discussing it at a teahouse.

一、课文　Text

🎧₁ （一）

服务员：几位来点儿什么？①

陆雨平：来一壶茶，再来一些点心。

服务员：好的，请稍等。

陆雨平：这就是我常说的老茶馆。今天
我把你们带到茶馆来，你们可
以了解一下我们这儿的风俗。

马大为：茶馆里人不少，真热闹。

林　娜：他们说话的声音太大了。

服务员：茶——来——了！您几位请慢
用。②

马大为：我们正在说声音大，这位服务员的声音更大。

王小云：茶馆就是最热闹的地方。有的人还把舞台搬进茶馆来了，在
茶馆里唱戏，比这儿还热闹呢。

林　娜：我觉得，在公共场所说话的声音
应该小一点儿。来中国以后，我
发现在不少饭馆、商店或者车站，人们说话的声音都很大。

表达看法
Expressing one's opinion

说实在的，我真有点儿不习惯。

王小云：到茶馆来的人都喜欢热闹。大家一边喝茶，一边聊天儿。聊得高兴的时候，说话的声音就会越来越大。喜欢安静的人不会到茶馆来。他们常常到别的地方去，比如去咖啡馆。③

陆雨平：林娜说得对。在公共场所，有的人说话的声音太大了。

王小云：我想在这儿聊一会儿天儿，可是你们都觉得这儿太闹。好，咱们走吧。前边有一个公园，那儿人不多。咱们到那个公园去散散步。

马大为：好的。咱们一边散步，一边聊天儿。

生词 New Words

1. 入乡随俗*	rù xiāng suí sú	IE	When in Rome, do as the Romans do; to conform to local customs
入	rù	V	to enter, to go in/into
乡	xiāng	N	village
随	suí	V	to follow
俗	sú		custom
2. 服务员	fúwùyuán	N	waiter/waitress
服务	fúwù	V	to serve

---

* The Chinese characters in the list of New Words marked in different color are the characters that students are supposed to master.

3. 壶	hú	N	kettle, pot 茶壶，酒壶，咖啡壶，一壶茶，一壶水
4. 点心	diǎnxin	N	refreshments, pastry 一些点心，一斤点心，一种点心，一块点心
5. 稍	shāo	Adv	slightly, a little 请稍等，稍等一下，稍大一点儿
6. 茶馆	cháguǎn	N	teahouse 老茶馆，新茶馆
7. 了解	liǎojiě	V	to get to know, to find out 了解情况，了解学生，了解中国，向他了解
8. 风俗	fēngsú	N	custom 了解风俗，这儿的风俗，一样的风俗，不同的风俗
9. 热闹	rènao	A/V	bustling with noise and excitement; to liven up 热闹的地方，很热闹，喜欢热闹；热闹一下
闹	nào	A/V	noisy; to make a noise/racket 太闹；别闹了
10. 说话	shuōhuà	VO	to speak, to talk 喜欢说话，不太爱说话，说什么话，说一会儿话
11. 声音	shēngyīn	N	sound, voice 说话的声音，演奏的声音，他的声音，声音很大
声	shēng	N	sound, voice 大声，小声，轻声
12. 更	gèng	Adv	more 更热闹，更可爱，更方便，更倒霉，更坏，更了解，更要，更放心，更注意，更觉得
13. 最	zuì	Adv	most 最热闹，最有名，最辛苦，最便宜，最难，最喜欢，最想，最习惯，最着急，最感兴趣

14.	舞台	wǔtái	N	stage　京剧舞台，越剧舞台，在舞台上唱，在舞台上演奏
	舞	wǔ	N	dance　跳一个舞
	台	tái		stage, platform
15.	搬	bān	V	to move　搬东西，搬家，搬到这儿，搬进茶馆
16.	场所	chǎngsuǒ	N	place　公共场所，学习场所
17.	发现	fāxiàn	V	to find　发现问题，发现一件事儿
18.	一边……	yìbiān……		at the same time, simultaneously　一边喝茶，一边看书
	一边……	yìbiān……		
19.	聊天儿	liáotiānr	VO	to chat　跟朋友聊天儿，喜欢聊天儿，聊一会儿天儿
20.	安静	ānjìng	A	quiet　喜欢安静，安静的地方，更安静，最安静
	静	jìng	A	quiet
21.	比如	bǐrú	V	to give an example
22.	咖啡馆	kāfēiguǎn	N	cafe, coffee bar

注释　Notes

① 几位来点儿什么?

"What would you like to order?"

"几位" (a few, several) represents the approximate number of people.

The verb "来" is commonly used to replace a verb that has a more specific meaning in spoken language. The construction "来+NP (the receiver of the action)" is often employed to inquire about someone's needs or to request something from someone, in which "来" replaces the verbs such as "要" and "买". For example, "您来点儿什么?" (meaning "您要点儿什么?"), "来一壶茶" (meaning "要一壶茶"), "来一斤蛋糕" (meaning "买一斤蛋糕").

② 您几位请慢用。

"Please enjoy it."

In "您 + Num + 位", "您" replaces "你们" ("您们" is not used in spoken language). "用" in "请慢用" is the polite expression of the verb like "吃" or "喝" used to show courtesy and respect. For example, 请用茶, 请用饭, 请用菜, 请用咖啡.

③ 他们常常到别的地方去，比如去咖啡馆。

"They often go to other places, such as a cafe."

The verb "比如" (also "比如说" in spoken language) is employed by a speaker when giving an example. It is usually placed at the end or in the middle of a sentence. For example,

他很喜欢吃中国菜，比如说烤鸭、涮羊肉。

有些公共场所，比如饭馆、车站，人们说话的声音太大，她很不习惯。

🎧2 （二）

丁力波：我们把自己的看法说出来，你们会不高兴吗？

陆雨平：当然不会。我们常跟外国朋友在一起，知道不同国家的人有不同的习惯。对我们来说，这很正常。④

丁力波：不了解外国文化的人会怎么想呢？

王小云：有些事儿他们会觉得很不习惯。比如说，中国人吃饭用筷子，西方人吃饭用刀叉。西方人把食物放在自己的盘子里，把大块切成小块，再把它送到嘴里。如果手指上有点儿食物，就舔手指，有的中国人看了也很不习惯。

举例说明
Giving an example

马大为：用刀叉吃饭，把手指上的食物舔干净，那是我们的好习惯。力波，你说是不是？

丁力波：是啊。我们从小到大都这样做。⑤

王小云：可是在我们这儿，吃饭的时候舔手指不是好习惯。

陆雨平：我看应该入乡随俗。⑥ 我们在国外的公共场所说话的声音要
小一点儿；你们到中国人家里吃饭也不一定要舔手指。

丁力波：对，我就是入乡随俗：吃中餐的时候，我用筷子；吃西餐的
时候，我用刀子、叉子。我觉得都很好。我爸爸妈妈他们也
都是这样。

王小云：力波，把"入乡随俗"翻译成英语，该怎么说？

生词 New Words

1. 看法	kànfǎ	N	view	自己的看法，大家的看法，对茶馆的看法，一种看法，有看法，看法不同
2. 正常	zhèngcháng	A	normal	正常的看法，正常的习惯，情况很正常
3. 筷子	kuàizi	N	chopsticks	用筷子吃饭，会用筷子，一双(shuāng)筷子
4. 刀叉	dāochā	N	knife and fork	用刀叉吃饭，习惯用刀叉，一副（fù）刀叉
刀（子）	dāo (zi)	N	knife	
叉（子）	chā (zi)	N	fork	
5. 食物	shíwù	N	food	买食物，拿食物，把食物放在桌子上
食	shí	V	to eat	
物	wù		thing	
6. 盘子	pánzi	N	plate, dish	新盘子，脏盘子，把食物放在盘子里
盘	pán	M	dish	一盘菜，一盘点心

7. 块	kuài	M	piece, lump 两块蛋糕，一小块苹果，一大块羊肉，一块点心
8. 切	qiē	V	to cut, to slice 切蛋糕，切苹果，切羊肉，把食物切成小块
9. 嘴	zuǐ	N	mouth 送到嘴里，吃到嘴里，一张嘴
10. 手指	shǒuzhǐ	N	finger 用手指，一个手指
手	shǒu	N	hand 左手，右手，用手，手里
11. 舔	tiǎn	V	to lick 舔食物，舔手指
12. 干净	gānjìng	A	clean 更干净，最干净，干净的衣服，干净的刀叉，干净的盘子，洗干净，舔干净
13. 这样	zhèyàng	Pr	so, such 这样做，这样写，这样切，这样干净，这样的照相机
14. 西餐	xīcān	N	Western-style food (meal) 吃西餐，对西餐感兴趣

补充生词 Supplementary Words

1. 相声	xiàngsheng	N	comic dialog
2. 老舍	Lǎo Shě	PN	Lao She (one of the modern Chinese writers)
3. 饮料	yǐnliào	N	drink
4. 保健品	bǎojiànpǐn	N	health care products
5. 精神	jīngshen	A	spirited
6. 片儿	piànr	N	slice
7. 蘸	zhàn	V	to dip
8. 敬	jìng	V	to offer politely
9. 香	xiāng	A	fragrant, sweet-smelling
10. 宋代	Sòngdài	PN	Song Dynasty

11.	苏东坡	Sū Dōngpō	PN	Su Dongpo (a famous Chinese writer of the Song Dynasty)
12.	寺庙	sìmiào	N	temple
13.	和尚	héshang	N	Buddhist monk
14.	书法家	shūfǎjiā	N	calligrapher
15.	胸	xiōng	N	chest
16.	阿弥陀佛	Ēmítuófó	N	merciful Buddha, May Buddha preserve us

注释　Notes

④ 对我们来说，这很正常。

"For us, it is a very common practice."

"对 + N + 来说" means to make a judgment from N's perspective ("N" indicating somebody or something). It is usually used at the beginning of a sentence. For example,

对丁力波来说，用筷子吃饭很容易。

对语言课本来说，课文和生词很重要。

⑤ 我们从小到大都这样做。

"We have been doing it since our childhood."

"从小到大" means "since one's childhood".

⑥ 我看应该入乡随俗。

"I think we should conform to the local customs."

The "看" in "我看" is similar to "想" or "觉得". It indicates a point of view or an opinion. For example,

我看现在走最好。

我看他今天不会来。

二、练习 Exercises

练习 与运用 **Drills and Practice** 3

核心句 KEY SENTENCES

1. 今天我把你们带到茶馆来。
2. 这位服务员的声音更大。
3. 茶馆就是最热闹的地方。
4. 大家一边喝茶，一边聊天儿。
5. 他们常常到别的地方去，比如去咖啡馆。
6. 咱们到那个公园去散散步。
7. 对我们来说，这很正常。
8. 西方人把食物放在自己的盘子里，把大块切成小块，再把它送到嘴里。
9. 把"入乡随俗"翻译成英语，该怎么说？

1. 熟读下列词组 Read the following phrases until you learn them by heart

（1）来一壶茶　　　　来一瓶葡萄酒　　　来一盘点心　　　来一份蛋糕
　　　来一个烤鸭　　　来一个涮羊肉　　　来一盘大虾　　　来一个蔬菜

（2）把包裹寄到美国去　　把汽车开到学校来　　把病人送到医院
　　　把桌子搬到宿舍里　　把蔬菜拿到厨房去　　把信寄到广州

（3）把衣服放在座位上　　把车停在邮局前边　　把刀叉拿在手里
　　　把生词记在本子上　　把练习写在纸上　　　把书丢在汽车里了

（4）把丝绸做成旗袍　　　把香蕉切成小块
　　　把中文翻译成英文　　把英镑换成人民币　　把"花儿"念成"画儿"了

（5）游一会儿泳　　化一会儿妆　　散一会儿步　　聊一会儿天儿　　帮一会儿忙

　　　游游泳　　　　化化妆　　　　散散步　　　　聊聊天儿　　　　帮帮忙

　　　游了游泳　　　化了化妆　　　散了散步　　　聊了聊天儿　　　帮了帮忙

（6）生活更方便　　　工作更辛苦　　　公园更安静　　　张三更高

　　　白车更漂亮　　　跑得更快　　　　做得更不好　　　写得更认真

　　　了解得更多　　　发现得更早　　　声音最大　　　　学习最努力

　　　服务最不热情　　变化最多　　　　时间最短　　　　提高得最快

　　　管理得最好　　　发展得最慢　　　搬得最重　　　　切得最小

2. 句型替换　Pattern drills

（1）A：你把你朋友带到哪儿去了？

　　　B：我把我朋友带到王府井去了。

这本词典	寄	西安
车	开	博物馆
桌子	搬	楼上
那个小孩儿	送	他家里
花儿	拿	温室里

（2）A：把衣服放在哪儿？

　　　B：把衣服放在床上吧。

筷子	放	桌上
自行车	放	楼下
问题	记	电脑里
今天的汉字	写	本子上
汽车	停	宿舍前边

（3）A：要把生日蛋糕切成小块吗？

　　　B：要切成小块。

刚买的布	做	衬衫
这篇课文	翻译	英语
听到的事儿	写	文章
人民币	换	英镑
这个地方	发展	城市

（4）A：这家咖啡馆比那家更安静。

　　　B：我看公园旁边的那家最安静。

黑车	红车	漂亮	白车
饭馆	咖啡馆	热闹	茶馆
这位服务员	那位	热情	我们学校的服务员
这个词	那个	正式	老师教的

（5）A：他们在做什么？

　　　B：他们一边散步，一边聊天儿。

洗衣服	听音乐
骑着自行车	说着、笑着
化妆	开玩笑
举办展览	卖画儿

（6）对我来说，不同的国家有不同的习惯，这很正常。

有些人	在茶馆里说话的声音很大
马大为他们	把手指上的食物舔干净
学生	有时候写错汉字
老师	有的问题不能回答

3. 课堂活动　Classroom activity

　　A student asks questions such as "在什么地方看书最好？" and "星期六的晚上你喜欢做什么？"; and then other students express their own opinions by using "我觉得", "我看", "我发现", "对我来说", "比如说", etc.

4. 会话练习　Conversation practice

> **会话常用语 IDIOMATIC EXPRESSIONS IN CONVERSATION**
>
> 对我们来说 (For us, ...)
>
> 比如说 (For example, ...)
>
> 你说是不是 (What do you think?)
>
> 我看 (In my opinion, I think...)

【表达看法　Expressing one's opinion】

（1）A：你觉得这儿的茶馆怎么样?

B：我觉得不错。几个朋友在一起喝喝茶、聊聊天儿，有时候还可以听听相声（xiàngsheng）、看看京剧，很有意思。

C：可是，我发现在这些场所人们说话的声音太大，不安静。

A：茶馆就是热闹的地方。人们说话的声音大，大家也都习惯了。特别是年轻人，聊天儿聊得高兴的时候，声音就越来越大了。

C：对我来说，公共场所应该安静点儿，说话的声音要小一点儿。这么闹，我觉得不舒服。

A：你的看法很对，我也是这样想的。听说一些茶馆，比如老舍（Lǎo Shě）茶馆，就很安静。

（2）A：你喜欢喝茶还是喝咖啡?

B：来中国以前我喜欢喝咖啡，现在入乡随俗，我也习惯喝茶了。中国人更喜欢喝茶，是不是?

A：可以这么说。一般中国人都爱喝茶。对我们来说，茶不但是一种饮料（yǐnliào），而且也是一种保健品（bǎojiànpǐn）。

B：你们把茶当成保健品?

A：是啊。我们觉得喝茶对身体很好。比如说，你吃得太多，觉得不舒服，喝点儿茶就好多了。

B：我看喝咖啡对身体也不错。工作累了的时候，喝杯咖啡，就有精神（jīngshen）了。

【举例说明 Giving an example】

A：来这儿以前，你了解中国文化吗？

B：了解一点儿。我是学中文的，对中国文化很感兴趣。比如说，我喜欢吃中餐、看中国电影、听中国民乐、参观中国画展览。你是什么时候注意西方文化的？

A：我考上英语系以后，就开始学习西方文学。我们这儿每天都能看到西方电影，图书馆也有很多英文书。我特别爱看英文小说。当然，要真正了解西方文化，还应该到西方国家去看一看。

5. 看图说话 Describe the following pictures

（1）

❶ 把……成……片儿（piànr）

❷ 把……在……

❸ 把……蘸（zhàn）上……

❹ 把……到……

（2）

❶ 把……在……

❷ 把……成……

❸ 把……在……

❹ 把……到……

6. 交际练习　Communication exercises

(1) While travelling abroad, you may have observed some customs different from yours. Describe some of them and state your opinions about them.

(2) Describe what you experienced when you tried to follow one of these foreign customs (or "doing as the Romans do").

After you speak, write down what you have said.

阅读与复述 Reading Comprehension and Paraphrasing

4 敬(jìng)香(xiāng)茶

宋代(Sòngdài)大文学家苏东坡(Sū Dōngpō)常常一个人出去旅行。他特别喜欢参观寺庙(sìmiào)。有一天,他走进一座寺庙。庙里的老和尚(héshang)看了看进来的这个人,觉得他是一个很普通的人,就坐着没动,只说了一个字:"坐。"又指了指小桌子上的茶壶,说:"茶。"

苏东坡就坐在小桌旁边。他和老和尚说了一会儿话,老和尚发现他知道的东西很多,就把他请到旁边的房间里,客气地说:"请坐!"又对小和尚说:"敬茶!"

又说了一会儿话,老和尚问苏东坡:"请问,您贵姓?"苏东坡说出了自己的名字。老和尚没想到,这位先生就是大文学家苏东坡。他马上把苏东坡请到最好的房间,很热情地说:"请上座!"而且还大声地对小和尚说:"快!快!敬香茶!"苏东坡笑着说:"不客气!"

老和尚知道,苏东坡不但是一位大文学家,而且还是一位大书法家(shūfǎjiā)。他想,如果请苏东坡给寺庙写一幅字,他们的寺庙就会更有名,这是一件大好事儿。想到这儿,他马上去房子里拿出一大张纸来,把它放在桌子上,再把两手放到胸(xiōng)前,嘴里说:"阿弥陀佛(Ēmítuófó)!阿弥陀佛!我想请您给我们写一幅字。"

苏东坡站起来,想了想,说:"可以。"他就把老和尚刚才说的话写在纸上:

坐,请坐,请上坐。

茶,敬茶,敬香茶。

老和尚站在旁边,一边看,一边念。念完这十二个字,他的脸红了。

三、语法　Grammar

1　"把"字句（3）　The "把" sentence (3)

The "把" sentences in this lesson contain a resultative complement, such as "到", "在" or "成", after the predicate verb. This kind of sentence is commonly used to express that an action causes something or somebody specific to change in position or state.

$$S + 把 + O_{把} + V + 到/在/成 + O$$

Subject	Predicate				
	把	O_把	V	到/在/成	O
我	把	你们	带	到	这儿。
陆雨平	把	汽车	开	到	宿舍楼前边。
西方人	把	食物	放	在	自己的盘子里。
丁力波	把	这些汉字	写	在	本子上。
他们	把	大块食物	切	成	小块。
你	把	这个词	翻译	成	英文。

Note:

In general, only the "把" sentences are used to express that an action causes something or somebody specific to change in position or state. For example, the above sentences cannot be stated as: "陆雨平开汽车到宿舍楼前边。" "西方人放食物在自己的盘子里。" "他翻译这个词成英文。"

2　副词"更""最"表示比较
The adverbs "更" and "最" used to express comparisons

The adverb "更" is used as an adverbial in front of an adjective, an optative verb or a verb denoting a psychological activity. It indicates a comparison between two things, or that of something under two situations. For example,

他比我更会游泳。(Compared with me)

这位服务员的声音更大。(Compared with other people's voice in the teahouse)

他现在<u>更不</u>想回家了。(Compared with the past)

The adverb "最" is used in comparison to show the superlative degree among a group of people or things.　It is often used as an adverbial before an adjective, an optative verb or a verb denoting a psychological activity. For example,

茶馆就是最热闹的地方。

我们年级有三个班，我们班的学生最多。

在他们几个人中，丁力波的汉字写得最漂亮。

马大为最爱听中国民乐。

3　离合词　Separable verbs

Some disyllabic verbs in the Chinese language are separable; one can insert other elements between them.　These verbs are called separable verbs.　The majority of separable verbs are composed of the "V + O" structure, such as "游泳，吃饭，起床，睡觉，开学，上课，发烧，看病，住院，开车，打的，罚款，过期，排队，化妆", which we have learned in previous lessons, and "说话、聊天儿" in this lesson.

他没有游过泳。

老师说了很长时间的话。

他在银行排了两次队。

我想在这儿聊一会儿天儿。

我朋友帮了我的忙。

Notes:

❶ Separable verbs usually cannot take objects. For example, you cannot say: "我朋友帮忙我。"

❷ Complements of duration or complements of frequency can only be used between, not after the two parts of a separable verb. For example, you cannot say: "老师说话了很长时间。" "他在银行排队了两次。"

The reduplicative form of a separable verb of the "V+O" structure is "AAB", "A—AB", or "A了AB". For example, "散散步，聊一聊天儿，游了游泳".

4 一边……, 一边…… The construction "一边……, 一边……"

"一边……, 一边……" ("…, at the same time…", "…while…") is used in front of verbs to indicate two or more actions taking place concurrently. For example,

咱们一边散步, 一边聊天儿。

王小云一边看小说, 一边听音乐。

四、字与词 Chinese Characters and Words

构词法 Word formation methods

Words in modern Chinese can be classified as simple words and compound words. Simple words are made up of one morpheme (generally speaking, one character). Compound words are composed of two or more morphemes. Grasping the formation method of a compound word is helpful for students to understand its meaning and learn new words. The following is one of the formation methods of compound words:

构词法（1）: 联合式
Word formation method (1): Coordinative compound words

Coordinative compound words usually take one of these three forms: "N+N" (e.g. 声音); "A+A"(e.g. 多少) and "V+V" (e.g. 考试) . They can also be divided into three types on the basis of the meaning of their components:

A. Words composed of the components with the same or similar meaning: 帮+助→帮助. For example,

　　休息　考试　聚会　管理　声音　语言

B. Words composed of the components with the opposite meaning: 东+西→东西. For example,

　　多少　没有　买卖　国家　左右　大小

C. Words composed of the components with the related meaning: 优+美→优美. For example,

　　安静　刀叉　学习　锻炼　教练　种类

Chinese Food Culture

Chinese people often say "food is heaven", meaning that food is the first necessity for common people. Over thousands of years, Chinese people have developed their unique food culture.

The most distinctive eating utensils in China are chopsticks, which were invented by ancient Chinese more than 3,000 years ago. Simple as they are, the chopsticks can perform a variety of functions, such as clamping, stirring, picking, raking and tearing, etc. There are quite a number of etiquette and taboos in using chopsticks. For instance, one cannot stick chopsticks into a bowl, or beat a bowl with chopsticks, or put food back into a plate after having picked it up. On a dinner table, when chopsticks are not used, they are supposed to be put neatly on the right side of the plate or bowl. Moreover, chopsticks are considered auspicious, implying the idea of "priority should be given to harmony" as they are always used in pairs.

Chinese cuisine also has a long history. Rich in varieties, it is divided into eight major styles in light of different regions. The dishes in different regions differ in their flavors, yet all of them emphasize the color, smell and taste. Chinese food is widely popular and Chinese restaurants are found in almost every part of the world.

Chinese people have been fond of drinking since ancient times. As drinking is a good way to relax and cheer up and dispel worries, people usually drink on family gatherings or dinner parties to liven up the atmosphere and keep up the friendship. Besides, Chinese people are famous for their hospitality. They like to propose toasts and urge their guests to drink more until they have drunk to their hearts' content.

China is the homeland of tea. Chinese people believe that drinking tea is good for both their physical and mental health. It is a decent social activity for friends to gather together to drink tea. Back in the Tang Dynasty, Chinese tea culture had already come into existence. Nowadays, Chinese people still like chatting with friends in a teahouse while sipping tea and appraising its flavor and quality.

第二十八课

Lesson

28

礼轻情意重

A small gift means a great deal.

Ding Libo and his friends celebrated the Mid-Autumn Festival with their Chinese friends for the first time. They ate moon cakes and enjoyed the bright full moon together. They also exchanged small gifts. Should presents be opened and praised right away? Once again, they found some differences in the conventions of their cultures.

一、课文 Text

🎧 5 (一)

陆雨平：今天是中秋节，① 中国人喜欢全家在一起过这个节日。今天，

我们也一起过。

马大为：谢谢你，雨平。今天我们可以了解一下中国人是怎么过中秋

节的。中秋节有春节那么热闹吗？

比较
Comparing

宋　华：中秋节虽然没有春节热闹，但是它也是

一个重要的节日。

王小云：我们准备了月饼、水果、茶、啤酒，咱们一边吃月饼，一边

赏月，怎么样？

丁力波：好啊！对了，我们还有一些小礼物要送给你们。

陆雨平：我们也要送给你们一些小礼物。

宋　华：我先来吧。力波，这是我给你的小纪念品，希望你喜欢。

丁力波：啊，是毛笔，文房四宝之一，② 还是名牌的呢！③ 这哪儿是小纪念品？这是一件大礼物。我要把它放在我的桌子上，每天都能看到它。

陆雨平：你不是喜欢中国书法吗？用了名牌毛笔，你的字一定会写得更好。

王小云：林娜，我给你带来了一件小礼物。你看看喜欢不喜欢。

林　娜：一条围巾，是丝绸的！太漂亮了！

馈赠与称赞
Presenting and appreciating a gift

丁力波：漂亮的林娜，戴上这条漂亮的围巾，就更漂亮了。

林　娜：是吗？我哪儿有你说的那么漂亮？小云，真谢谢你！对我来说，这是最好的礼物。

陆雨平：我没有更好的礼物送给大为，我知道他喜欢中国音乐，就送他一套音乐光盘。

马大为：你们看，我收到的礼物最好了，一套音乐光盘，是中国民乐！谢谢。

陆雨平：不客气，一点儿小意思。④

丁力波：该我们了吧？我们也有一些礼物送给你们。这是给宋华的。

宋　华：谢谢！

马大为：雨平，这是给你的。

陆雨平：非常感谢！

林　娜：小云，看看我给你的礼物。

王小云：谢谢你！

宋　华：大家都送完礼物了，我看，咱们该吃月饼了！

陆雨平：祝大家中秋快乐！干杯！

大　家：干杯！

王小云：快来看，月亮上来了。今天的月亮多美啊！

生词 New Words

1. 礼轻情意重	lǐ qīng qíngyì zhòng	IE	A small gift means a great deal.	
轻	qīng	A	light	
情意	qíngyì	N	affection	
2. 节日	jiérì	N	festival	过这个节日，重要的节日
3. 准备	zhǔnbèi	V	to prepare	准备礼物，准备西餐，准备考试，准备旅行
4. 月饼	yuèbing	N	moon cake	中秋月饼，准备月饼，切月饼，一个月饼，一块月饼
饼	bǐng	N	cake	
5. 水果	shuǐguǒ	N	fruit	便宜的水果，一斤水果，一种水果，水果的种类
6. 啤酒	píjiǔ	N	beer	喝啤酒，两瓶啤酒

7. 赏	shǎng	V	to enjoy 赏月，赏花儿，陪朋友赏花儿
8. 纪念品	jìniànpǐn	N	souvenir 送纪念品，买纪念品，小纪念品
纪念	jìniàn	V	to commemorate
品	pǐn	Suf	article, product
9. 希望	xīwàng	V/N	to hope; hope 希望你喜欢；有希望，希望很大
10. 毛笔	máobǐ	N	writing brush 用毛笔写字，用毛笔画画儿
毛	máo	N	hair, feather, down
11. 文房四宝	wénfáng sìbǎo	IE	the four treasures of the study
宝	bǎo	N	treasure
12. ……之一	……zhī yī		one of 文房四宝之一，有名的教授之一
13. 名牌	míngpái	N	famous brand 名牌毛笔，名牌衣服，名牌照相机
牌（子）	pái (zi)	N	brand 什么牌子，牌子很有名
14. 书法	shūfǎ	N	calligraphy 汉字书法，喜欢书法
15. 围巾	wéijīn	N	scarf 丝绸围巾，漂亮的围巾，白围巾，名牌围巾，一条围巾
围	wéi	V	to enclose
巾	jīn	N	a piece of cloth (used as a towel, scarf, kerchief, etc.)
16. 戴	dài	V	to put on, to wear 戴围巾
17. 那么	nàme	Pr	so, like that 那么漂亮，那么热闹，那么安静，那么干净
18. 收	shōu	V	to receive, to accept 收礼物，收信，收到明信片，收到他寄的书

19.	小意思	xiǎoyìsi	N	small token of affection 一点儿小意思
20.	干杯	gānbēi	VO	to drink a toast 请大家干杯
	干	gān	A	dry
	杯（子）	bēi (zi)	N	cup
21.	月亮	yuèliang	N	moon 月亮上来了
22.	中秋节	Zhōngqiū Jié	PN	Mid-Autumn Festival 过中秋节
23.	春节	Chūn Jié	PN	Spring Festival, Chinese New Year 春节快乐

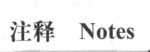 

注释 Notes

① 今天是中秋节。

"Today is the Mid-Autumn Festival."

See the introduction to the Mid-Autumn Festival and the Spring Festival in the "Cultural Note" of Lesson 20 in Textbook 2.

② 啊，是毛笔，文房四宝之一。

"Ah, it's a writing brush, one of the four treasures of the study."

"文房" is a study. People regarded the writing brush, ink, paper and inkstone as the four treasures of the study.

"之" in "之一" is a structural particle derived from the classical Chinese. Its usage is similar to "的" in modern Chinese. For example, 有名的画家之一，中国名牌之一，学习最好的学生之一，要回答的问题之一。

③ 还是名牌的呢！

"It's even a product of a famous brand!"

The adverb "还" (4) is used to indicate "something unexpected". It also means "even". When used with "呢", it adds a slightly surprised and exaggerated tone to the sentence. For example,

他的小女儿还会唱越剧呢！

月饼上还有画儿呢！

④ 不客气，一点儿小意思。

　　"You are welcome. This is just a small gift."

　　"小意思" means "small token of affection." This is a polite expression one uses when presenting a gift to someone.

🎧 6　（二）

马大为：我们第一次过中国的中秋节，又收到了那么好的礼物，大家都很高兴。不过，我有个问题想问问你。⑤

宋　华：什么问题？

马大为：我们收到礼物，就马上把它打开，看看是什么。你们拿到礼物以后，只看看外边，不打开，好像没有我们那么想知道里边是什么。这是为什么？

宋　华：我先问你，收到礼物的时候，你们为什么要马上打开看呢？

马大为：我们把礼物打开看，称赞礼物，表示感谢，这是尊重送礼物的人。当然，也希望自己能得到一种惊喜。你们的习惯我就不懂了，你们不喜欢别人给你们礼物吗？

王小云：当然不是。朋友送的礼物怎么会不喜欢呢？我们收到朋友的礼物，一般不马上打开看，这也是尊重送礼物的人。我们觉得送什么礼物不重要。人们常说"礼轻情意重"，重要的是友谊。

> 反语
> **Asking in retort**

马大为：是这样！⑥ 说真的，那天你们没有打开，我们还有点儿担心呢。

王小云：担心什么？

马大为：担心你们不喜欢我们的礼物。

宋 华：你说到哪儿去了？⑦你们送的礼物都很好。比如说，丁力波送

的加拿大糖，不是很有特色吗？我们都很喜欢。

丁力波：你们都很喜欢，我太高兴了。

生词 New Words

1. 不过	búguò	Conj	however, but
2. 称赞	chēngzàn	V	to praise, to compliment 称赞礼物，称赞林娜
3. 表示	biǎoshì	V/N	to express; expression 表示喜欢，表示感兴趣，表示放心；热情的表示，正常的表示
4. 感谢	gǎnxiè	V	to thank 感谢朋友，感谢你的帮助，非常感谢，表示感谢
5. 尊重	zūnzhòng	V	to respect 尊重老师，尊重送礼的人，尊重这儿的风俗，尊重他们的习惯，尊重他的看法，表示尊重
6. 得到	dédào	V	to get 得到礼物，得到纪念品，得到帮助，得到称赞，得到尊重
7. 惊喜	jīngxǐ	N	pleasant surprise 得到惊喜，给他一个惊喜
惊	jīng	V	to surprise
喜	xǐ		to be happy

8.	别人	biéren	Pr	other people　告诉别人，感谢别人，尊重别人，别人的帮助，别人的礼物
9.	一般	yìbān	A	general, ordinary　一般的问题，一般的看法，一般的小说，一般的演员，一般的朋友，一般觉得，一般喜欢
10.	重要	zhòngyào	A	important　重要的场所，重要的发现，重要的特点，重要的看法，重要的生词
11.	友谊	yǒuyì	N	friendship　重要的是友谊，我们的友谊
12.	担心	dānxīn	VO	to worry　担心什么，担心天气，担心太闹，担心你们不喜欢，有点儿担心
13.	糖	táng	N	sweets, candy　糖块，白糖，红糖，放不放糖，放一点儿糖
14.	特色	tèsè	N	characteristic, feature　（没）有特色，南方特色，农村特色，中国特色

补充生词 Supplementary Words

1.	美的	Měidí	PN	a famous brand of electric instrument in China
2.	华山	Huà Shān	PN	a famous mountain in Shaanxi Province of China
3.	量	liáng	V	to measure
4.	矮	ǎi	A	short
5.	破费	pòfèi	V	to spend money
6.	嫦娥奔月	Cháng'é bèn yuè	IE	Chang'e flew to the moon
	嫦娥	Cháng'é	PN	Chang'e (a goddness lived in the Lunar Palace)
7.	唐朝	Tángcháo	PN	Tang Dynasty
8.	古代	gǔdài	N	ancient times

9. 神话	shénhuà	N	fairy tale
10. 月宫	yuègōng	N	the Lunar Palace
11. 仙女	xiānnǚ	N	goddess, immortal maiden
12. 原来	yuánlái	N	formerly, originally
13. 人间	rénjiān	N	the human world
14. 闻	wén	V	to smell
15. 唐明皇	Táng Mínghuáng	PN	Emperor Tangminghuang(an emperor of the Tang Dynasty)
16. 皇宫	huánggōng	N	imperial palace
17. 醒	xǐng	V	to wake up
18. 团聚	tuánjù	V	to reunite

注释　Notes

⑤ 不过，我有个问题想问问你。

"However, I have a question for you."

"不过" is a conjunction that expresses a turn in a conversation and connects the clauses. It is often used to supplement or modify what is mentioned above and is followed by a pause. "不过" suggests a milder transition in tone than "但是" or "可是", and is also often used in spoken Chinese. For example,

昨天大家都玩儿得很好。不过，我有个问题想问问你。

好像要下大雨，不过不会马上下。

他很喜欢玩儿，不过学习还可以。

⑥ 是这样！

"That's why!"

"是这样", spoken with emphasis on "这样", shows the realization of the occurrence of something. For example,

A：林娜怎么会被撞伤呢?

B：林娜骑自行车往右拐的时候没有注意，撞到了停在路边的车上。

A：是这样！

⑦ 你说到哪儿去了?

"What are you talking about?"

It is used to politely refute someone's point of view. For example,

A：昨天我没有来，你们不会不高兴吧？

B：你说到哪儿去了？我们知道你很忙。

二、练习 Exercises

练习与运用 Drills and Practice

核心句 KEY SENTENCES

1. 中秋节有春节那么热闹吗？
2. 中秋节没有春节热闹。
3. 我们还有一些礼物送给你们。
4. 这哪儿是小纪念品？
5. 是毛笔，文房四宝之一，还是名牌的呢！
6. 漂亮的林娜，戴上这条漂亮的围巾，就更漂亮了。
7. 我们收到礼物，就马上把它打开。
8. 朋友送的礼物怎么会不喜欢呢？
9. 加拿大糖不是很有特色吗？

1. 熟读下列词组 Read the following phrases until you learn them by heart

（1）没有他弟弟高　　　　没有那辆车漂亮　　　　没有那个乐曲感人

　　没有我们辛苦　　　　没有那套西服贵　　　　没有现在的教练有名

　　没有这儿干净　　　　没有这个小伙子帅　　　　没有他们小区方便

　　　　没有她那么倒霉　　　没有他那么爱聊天儿　　　没有他们那么高兴
　　　　没有他那么担心　　　有没有北京这么冷　　　　有没有这套房子大
（2）没有我们来得早　　　没有林娜穿得漂亮　　　　没有他们准备得好
　　　　没有我罚款罚得多　　没有司机开车开得好　　　没有他看书看得多
（3）戴上围巾　　　穿上旗袍　　　带上借书证　　　拿上照相机
　　　　填上职业　　　画上花儿　　　包上红纸　　　写上他的名字
（4）打开书　　　打开电视　　　打开红葡萄酒　　　打开包裹　　开开门
　　　　切开蛋糕　　切开月饼　　切开水果　　　　　打开词典　　搬开床
（5）有东西吃　　　有衣服穿　　　有事情做　　　　有纪念品送给你们
　　　　有一个问题问老师　　没有报看　　　　没有房子住
　　　　没有啤酒喝　　　　没有自行车骑　　没有西餐吃
（6）有名的医生之一　　　很好的同学之一　　　主要的大学之一
　　　　参加比赛的学生之一　　要回答的问题之一　　喜欢看的小说之一
　　　　感兴趣的问题之一

2. 句型替换　Pattern drills

（1）A：那种笔有这种笔好吗？
　　　B：那种笔有这种笔好。

他妹妹	他弟弟	高
他买的车	那辆车	漂亮
他租的房子	这套房子	大
那儿的冬天	北京这么	冷

（2）A：中秋节有没有春节那么热闹？
　　　B：中秋节没有春节那么热闹。

这套西服	那套西服	贵
那个乐曲	这个乐曲	感人
我们这儿	他们小区	方便
以前的教练	现在的教练	有名

（3）A：我不知道<u>怎么用毛笔写字</u>。

　　　B：你不是<u>学过中国书法</u>吗?

老茶馆怎么样	觉得那儿太闹
兵马俑有多大	去过西安
怎么介绍中国画	画过很多中国画
那位小姐是谁	去年见过她一次

（4）A：我担心你们<u>不喜欢我们的礼物</u>。

　　　B：<u>朋友送的礼物</u>，怎么会<u>不喜欢</u>呢?

不来参加这个聚会	你们请我们来	不参加
不习惯这儿的生活	我们已经"中国化"了	不习惯
忘了出发的时间	昨天刚刚告诉我们	忘了
觉得那儿没有意思	这么好的展览	觉得没意思

（5）A：你现在忙不忙?

　　　B：很忙。我有很多<u>练习要做</u>。

语法	复习
课文	翻译
文章	写
事儿	做
考试	准备

（6）A：<u>他戴上那条丝绸围巾了</u>没有?

　　　B：没有，<u>今天不冷</u>。

穿	那套新西服	今天不用穿得很正式
带	借书证	他不去图书馆
拿	照相机	那儿不能拍照
写	他的名字	他说要想一想

（7）A：他们让你做什么？

　　　B：让我把礼物 打开。

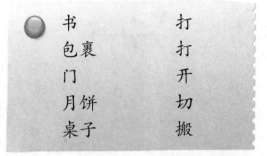

书	打
包裹	打
门	开
月饼	切
桌子	搬

（8）A：你知道毛笔吗？

　　　B：知道。毛笔是文房四宝之一。

中秋节	中国几个重要的节日
齐白石	中国有名的画家
美的（Měidí）	中国名牌
华山（Huà Shān）	中国有名的大山
《红楼梦》	中国有名的古典小说
《春江花月夜》	中国有名的古典乐曲

3. 课堂活动　Classroom activities

(1) Student A makes a sentence, and Student B speaks another sentence to make a slight transition in meaning by using "不过". For example,

　　　A：我明天不去借书了。

　　　B：不过我还得去图书馆查查新课本。

(2) Student A says a sentence, and Student B supplements it with another sentence containing the construction "还……呢" to express surprise and exaggeration. For example,

　　　A：他在北京一年就学了很多东西。

　　　B：他还会打太极拳呢！

4. 会话练习　Conversation practice

> **会话常用语 IDIOMATIC EXPRESSIONS IN CONVERSATION**
>
> 这是为什么 (Why is this/that?)
>
> 当然不是 (Of course not.)
>
> 是这样 (That's why.)
>
> 你说到哪儿去了 (What are you talking about?)

【比较　Comparing】

（1）A：我知道那种电脑是名牌的，这种电脑有那种好吗?

　　　B：说实在的，这种电脑不一定没有那种好，而且还比那种便宜几百块钱。

　　　A：是这样! 不过我喜欢名牌。我觉得买名牌的好。

（2）A：我想做一件旗袍，要做丝绸的。

　　　B：好，我给你量（liáng）一量。

　　　A：这件旗袍不是给我自己做的，是给我姐姐做的。

　　　B：你姐姐有没有你这么高?

　　　A：她没有我高，她比我矮（ǎi）两公分。我的衣服她也能穿。

　　　B：好了，一个星期以后来取。请到那边交钱。

【馈赠与称赞　Presenting and appreciating a gift】

（1）A：这是我给你的小纪念品，希望你喜欢。

　　　B：是中国音乐光盘，太感谢你了! 对我来说，这是最好的礼物。

　　　A：哪里，一点儿小意思。

（2）A：我给你带来了一件小礼物。

　　　B：绿茶，太好了! 我最爱喝中国绿茶。真谢谢你。

　　　A：不客气。你喜欢我就很高兴。

（3）A：我这次从上海回来，给朋友们带了点儿小礼物。这是给你的，不知道你喜欢不喜欢。

B：上海衬衫，还是名牌的呢！你太客气了，让你破费（pòfèi），

真不好意思。

A：你说到哪儿去了？这只是一点儿小意思。

【反诘 Asking in retort】

（1）A：我明天不去听音乐会了。

B：你昨天不是说要跟我们一起去吗？票已经买好了，为什么又不

去了？

（2）A：我觉得天气越来越热了。

B：今天气温只有26度，哪儿热啊？

（3）A：昨天晚上你怎么不跟他们一起过中秋节？

B：我不知道这事儿。

C：你怎么会不知道呢？是王小云在图书馆告诉咱们的。

【担心 Worrying】

A：他昨天没有来，我真有点儿担心了。

B：担心什么？

A：我担心他病了。

5. 看图说话 Describe the following pictures

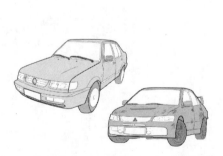

（跟……一样　比……　没有……　有……　更……　最……）

6. 交际练习 Communication exercises

(1) When receiving a gift from one of your Chinese friends, what should you say?

(2) When giving your Chinese friend a gift, what should you say?

(3) When receiving a gift from one's friend, one culture emphasizes the value of the gift by praising it to show that it is greatly appreciated. Another culture emphasizes the kindness of the gift-giver by expressing the receiver's feelings that the gift is too much for him. Discuss the similarities and differences between these two practices.

After you speak, write down what you have said.

阅读与复述 Reading Comprehension and Paraphrasing

8 嫦娥奔月（Cháng'é Bèn Yuè）

中秋节赏月的风俗是从唐朝（Tángcháo）开始的。

在中国古代（gǔdài）神话（shénhuà）中，月亮上有一个月宫（yuègōng），那儿有一位很美的仙女（xiānnǚ），她的名字叫嫦娥。嫦娥原来（yuánlái）是人间（rénjiān）的女子，她丈夫得到一种特别的药，交给了她。一天，嫦娥闻（wén）了闻这个药，就觉得自己身体变轻了，飞起来了。她飞得越来越高，越来越快，最后就飞到月亮上去了。嫦娥成了月宫里的仙女。

传说在一个八月十五的晚上，唐朝的皇帝唐明皇（Táng Mínghuáng）

做了一个梦，梦见自己来到了月宫。他觉得他的皇宫（huánggōng）没有月宫这么安静，这么高大。他在月宫里见到了嫦娥。漂亮的嫦娥穿着白色的衣服，非常热情地请唐明皇喝酒，还为他唱歌跳舞。唐明皇以前没有听过这么好听的歌，也没有看过这么美的舞。他醒（xǐng）了以后，就把这个梦写成了一首有名的乐曲。从那以后，每年的八月十五，唐明皇都要在皇宫里举办赏月的音乐会，演奏他写的这首乐曲。后来，中秋节就成了中国的一个节日。这一天，全家人要团聚（tuánjù）在一起，一边吃月饼，一边赏月。中秋节人们看月亮的时候，好像还能看到一点儿嫦娥住的月宫呢！

三、语法　Grammar

1 用动词"有/没有"表示比较
Using the verb "有/没有" to express comparisons

The construction "X+有/没有+Y+A" is used to indicate whether the quality or characteristic of something ("X") is as much as that of another thing ("Y"). This type of comparison uses the second object as the criterion. The result of the comparison is often expressed by an adjective.

S＋有/没有＋NP（＋这么/那么）＋A

Subject	Predicate					
	Adv	有/没有	NP	（这么/那么）	A	Pt
中秋节		有	春节	那么	热闹	吗？
中秋节		没有	春节	那么	热闹。	
那种笔		没有	这种笔		好。	
我		没有	你说的	那么	漂亮。	
妹妹		有没有	姐姐	这么	高？	
妹妹	已经	有	姐姐	这么	高	了。

The quality or characteristic of the comparison can also be expressed with a verb phrase.

Subject	Predicate			
	有/没有	NP	（这么/那么）	VP
他	有没有	你	那么	喜欢书法？
他	没有	我	那么	喜欢书法。
我	没有	你		跑得快。
我们	没有	你们		用刀叉用得好。
你们	没有	我们	那么	想知道里边是什么。

Note:

The negative form of the comparative sentence with the structure of "有/没有" ("X+没有+Y+A/ VP") is more commonly used, and it is often found in declarative sentences. Its affirmative form "X+ 有+Y+A/VP" is less frequently used, and it is often found in interrogative sentences and answers to them.

2 反问句（1）　The rhetorical question (1)

Some interrogative sentences are actually not used to ask questions, but to emphasize certain obvious reasons or facts.

A. The construction "不是……吗" is used to emphasize an affirmation. For example,

大为不是美国人吗？（是美国人）

你不是喜欢中国书法吗？（是喜欢中国书法）

加拿大糖不是很有特色吗？（是很有特色）

你不是参观过美术馆吗？（是参观过美术馆）

B. Interrogative pronouns are used to emphasize an affirmation or a negation. For example,

这哪儿是小纪念品？（这不是小纪念品）

我哪儿有你说的那么漂亮？（我没有你说的那么漂亮）

朋友送的礼物怎么会不喜欢呢？（朋友送的礼物当然喜欢）

3 连动句（3）　Sentences with serial verb phrases (3)

In some of the sentences with serial verb phrases, the first verb is "有/没有", and its object is also the receiver of the action described by the second verb. The second verb does not have a direct object.

$$S + （Adv+）有/没有 + O + V_2$$

Subject	Predicate			
	Adv	有/没有	O	V₂
他	现在	没有	书	看。
学生们	星期天	有	很多练习	要做。
我们		有	一些小礼物	要送给你们。
我		没有	更好的礼物	送给大为。
我		有	一个问题	想问问你。

4 结果补语"上、开"　"上" and "开" as the resultative complements

The verb "上" can be used as a resultative complement to indicate that separate things are joined together, or one thing is attached to another. For example, "关上门，戴上围巾，写上名字，带上护照".

The verb "开" can be used as a resultative complement to indicate that integrated or joined things are separated. For example, "打开礼物，打开书，切开苹果，搬开桌子".

四、字与词　Chinese Characters and Words

构词法（2）：偏正式

Word formation method (2): Modifier-modified compound words

In such a structure, the first word modifies or restricts the latter one, e.g. 月+饼→月饼.

Other examples,

茶馆	爱情	蛋糕	西餐	中餐	汽车	火车	毛笔	电脑	电视
厨房	花园	剧院	客厅	礼物	商店	小孩儿	农民	工人	医生
医院	阳台	围巾	名牌	以前	春天	今年	羊肉	蔬菜	外国
名片	油画	音乐	汉语	生词	邮费				

文化知识 Cultural Note

Chinese Culture of Gift-Giving

Chinese people take human relations very seriously. For them, gift-giving is an important way to show respect and maintain relationships. They believe that "a small gift means a great deal". Therefore, what matters is not the price of the gift, but the friendly feelings embodied in it.

One should bear the receiver and the occasion in mind when giving a gift. When you are visiting someone's family, fruits and local specialties are good choices for a gift, or you may bring some toys or candies for the children or health care products for the elderly. Of course you may also choose a gift according to the receiver's preference. A gift is usually given face to face. If it is a birthday or wedding gift, a card is supposed to be attached, with congratulations and the giver's name written on it.

It is a fashion in China today to give a red packet as a gift. A red packet is a red paper bag with blessings written on its surface and cash in it. Red packets are given to children on the Spring Festival as the "lucky money", or to newly-weds, newly-parents or people who have just moved to a new residence as cash gifts for them to buy what they need.

Chinese people seldom open the package of a gift immediately after receiving it. They usually accept the gift, saying "thank you" to the giver, and then put it aside. They won't open it until the giver has left. This shows their respect for the giver, as gifts may differ in prices, but the friendly feelings contained in them do not.

There are also some taboos in gift-giving. For example, there is a Chinese saying that "good things come in pairs", so gifts for happy occasions had better be given in even numbers, except for the number "4", whose Chinese pronunciation resembles that of "death" in Chinese. As for colors, white and black are to be avoided, since the former indicates sorrow and the latter signifies disaster and mourning. Chinese people like the color of red best. They think red is the symbol of happiness, peace and festivity. Other taboo gifts include a clock ("to give a clock to someone" is pronounced the same as "to escort someone to the grave" in Chinese) and pears, which cannot be given to couples or lovers (since "pear" is homophonous to "separate" in Chinese).

第二十九课

Lesson

29

请多提意见

Your suggestions will be highly appreciated.

"Modesty" is always regarded as a virtue in the Chinese culture. Professor Zhang says that his calligraphy is "just so so". He also asks his young students to make suggestions for his newly published book. Do you know why?

一、课文　Text

9　（一）

张教授：你们来了！欢迎，欢迎！快请进。

林　娜：张教授，这是给您的花儿。

张教授：谢谢。你们太客气了。请坐，喝点儿什么？

林　娜：喝茶吧。您的书房很有特色：墙上挂着中国字画，书架上放着这么多古书，桌上放着文房四宝，外边还整整齐齐地摆着这么多花儿，还有盆景呢。这些花儿真漂亮，都是您种的吗？

描述事物
Describing something

张教授：不，都是买的。不过它们在我这儿长得越来越好，现在也开花儿了。

丁力波：这叫君子兰吧？长长的绿叶，红红的花儿，真好看。

张教授：是叫君子兰。① 这种花儿很好养，② 开花儿的时间也比较长。

林　娜：养花儿真有意思。我明天下了课就去买盆花儿，③ 摆在宿舍里。我也有花儿养了。

马大为：养花儿是有意思，可是你能养好吗？

林 娜：当然能养好！我看，养花儿没有学汉语那么难吧。

张教授：养花儿是不太难。不过，要把花儿养好，那就不容易了。人们常说"姑娘爱花儿"，林娜喜欢养花儿，我想她一定能养好。

林 娜：谢谢，张教授，我也是这样想的。

丁力波：这些盆景都是您自己的作品吧？

张教授：是的。工作累了的时候，我就到外边去浇浇花儿，把这些盆景修整修整。这是很好的休息。

强调肯定
Emphasizing an affirmation

丁力波：盆景是一种艺术，听说，种盆景很不容易。张教授，您还真是一位园艺师呢！

张教授：我哪儿是园艺师？这只是一点儿爱好。

生词 New Words

1. 意见	yìjiàn	N	idea, suggestion 提意见，请多提意见，有意见，好意见
2. 欢迎	huānyíng	V	to welcome 欢迎你们，欢迎参观，欢迎多提意见
3. 书房	shūfáng	N	study

4.	墙	qiáng	N	wall 墙上
5.	挂	guà	V	to hang 挂照片，挂画儿，挂在墙上，墙上挂着
6.	字画	zìhuà	N	calligraphy and painting 有名的字画，墙上挂着字画，一幅字画
	*字	zì	N	character, handwriting 张教授的字，我的字，这幅字
7.	书架	shūjià	N	bookshelf 放在书架上，书架上放着书
8.	古书	gǔshū	N	ancient book 书架上有很多古书，书架上放着古书
	古	gǔ	A	ancient 古人，古时候
9.	整齐	zhěngqí	A	neat, tidy 整齐的书架，衣服放得整齐，站得很整齐，整整齐齐
10.	地	de	Pt	*used to form an adverbial adjunct* 整整齐齐地放着，高高兴兴地聊天儿，很好地复习，更多地练习
11.	摆	bǎi	V	to put, to place 摆在桌上，摆在外边，摆在宿舍里，摆着花儿，整整齐齐地摆着
12.	盆景	pénjǐng	N	miniature trees and rockery in a pot, bonsai 中国盆景，摆着盆景，种盆景
	盆	pén	N	a container made of plastic or clay for growing plants in 花盆
13.	长	zhǎng	V	to grow 花儿长得很好，蔬菜长得很快，小狗长得很大，小孩儿长得很高
14.	开花儿	kāihuār	VO	to bloom 现在开花儿了，让它常开花儿
15.	君子兰	jūnzǐlán	N	kaffir lily

16. 叶（子）	yè (zi)	N	leaf　君子兰的叶子，绿叶
17. 好看	hǎokàn	A	pleasant to look at, good-looking　真好看，好看的花儿，好看的姑娘，好看的小说，好看的电影
18. 养	yǎng	V	to grow, to raise　养花儿，养狗，养鸭，养羊，养大，养好，不好养的花儿
19. 比较	bǐjiào	Adv/V	comparatively, quite; to compare　比较长，比较重，比较热闹，比较干净，比较整齐，比较好看，比较好养；比较一下，和他比较
20. 人们	rénmen	N	people　人们常说，这里的人们
21. 作品	zuòpǐn	N	work of literature or art　文学作品，美术作品，盆景作品，书法作品，重要的作品，一般的作品，主要作品，感人的作品，自己的作品
22. 浇	jiāo	V	to water　浇花儿，浇水
23. 修整	xiūzhěng	V	to prune, to trim　修整盆景
24. 艺术	yìshù	N	art　盆景艺术，书法艺术，艺术作品，爱好艺术
25. 园艺师	yuányìshī	N	horticulturist　当园艺师，成了园艺师
园艺	yuányì	N	gardening　喜欢园艺，爱好园艺
师	shī	Suf	person skillful at a certain profession, expert, master　医师，工程师

注释　Notes

① 是叫君子兰。

"It is indeed called kaffir lily."

When "是" is used before a verbal predicate, an adjectival predicate, or a predicate of subject-predicate phrase, it means "indeed". It emphasizes and confirms the previous sentence and should be stressed. For example,

A：养花儿真有意思。

B：养花儿是有意思。

A：养花儿没有学汉语那么难吧?

B：养花儿是不太难。

A：听说他学习很努力。

B：他是学习很努力。

② 这种花儿很好养。

"This kind of flower is very easy to grow."

The adjective "好" is followed by a verb to express the meaning of "it is easy to do something". Here, "好" means "easy". The negative form of this structure is "不好＋V". For example,

这篇文章好懂。

太极拳好学。

今天的练习不好做。

③ 我明天下了课就去买盆花儿。

"I'll buy a pot of flower right after class tomorrow."

The adverb "就" (4) often connects two verbs or verbal phrases (with the particle "了" usually added to the first one) and suggests that the second action takes place right after the first one. For example,

他吃了饭就来了。

他们到了医院就给他打电话。

🎧 10 （二）

丁力波：张教授，我很喜欢中国书法，也跟老师学过，可是进步不快。我不知道该怎么办？

张教授：学习书法要多看、多练。人们常说，如果你每天都认认真真地练，不用一百天，就能把汉字写得很漂亮。当然，要把汉字写成书法艺术作品，还要更多地练习。

丁力波：张教授，我想请您给我写一幅字，不知道行不行？

张教授：我的字很一般，你应该多看书法家的字。

丁力波：我知道您的书法很有名。这幅字能给我吗？

张教授：这幅字被我写坏了。我今天刚写了一幅，你看上边写着什么？

丁力波："弟子不必不如师，师不必贤于弟子。"④ 张教授，请问，这个句子是什么意思？

张教授：这是唐代一位文学家说过的话，意思是，学生不一定不如老师，老师也不一定比学生高明。老师和学生应该互相学习。

丁力波：谢谢您，张教授。这幅字很有意思，我要把它挂在我宿舍的墙上。

张教授：对了，这是我刚写的一本书，送给你们，每人一本。我已经
把你们的名字写上了，请多提意见。⑤

马大为：是《汉字书法艺术》，谢谢您。张
教授，您太谦虚了。您是老师，我们才学了这么一点儿中
文，怎么能提出意见呢？

张教授：那位唐代文学家是怎么说的？"弟子不必不如师，师不必贤
于弟子。"

> 表示谦虚
> **Expressing modesty**

生词 New Words

1. 练	liàn	V	to practice	练字，练书法，练太极拳，练京剧，练汉语，练中国画，多练，认认真真地练
2. 书法家	shūfǎjiā	N	calligrapher	
*家	jiā	Suf	specialist in a certain field	艺术家，美术家，音乐家，画家，小说家
3. 弟子不必不如师	dìzǐ búbì bùrú shī	IE	Disciples are not necessarily inferior to their teachers.	
弟子	dìzǐ	N	disciple, student	
不必	búbì	Adv	not necessarily	
不如	bùrú	V	to be not as good as, to be inferior to	我不如他，学生不一定不如老师
4. 师不必贤于弟子	shī búbì xián yú dìzǐ	IE	Teachers are not necessarily wiser than their disciples.	
贤	xián		virtuous, able	
5. 句子	jùzi	N	sentence	一个句子，汉语句子
句	jù	M	*used of language*	两句话

6. 意思	yìsi	N	meaning 句子的意思，生词的意思，课文的意思，文章的意思，我的意思，什么意思
7. 文学家	wénxuéjiā	N	writer 有名的文学家
8. 高明	gāomíng	A	brilliant, wise 高明的老师，高明的画家，很高明
9. 互相	hùxiāng	Adv	mutually, each other 互相学习，互相帮助，互相介绍，互相祝贺，互相比较
10. 谦虚	qiānxū	A	modest 谦虚的人，太谦虚了，谦虚地说
11. 唐代	Tángdài	PN	Tang Dynasty 唐代文学家，唐代画家

补充生词 Supplementary Words

1. 电视机	diànshìjī	N	TV set
2. 柜子	guìzi	N	cupboard
3. 沙发	shāfā	N	sofa
4. 时装	shízhāng	N	fashion
5. 皮包	píbāo	N	leather handbag
6. 眼睛	yǎnjing	N	eye
7. 鼻子	bízi	N	nose
8. 讨论	tǎolùn	V	to discuss
9. 参考	cānkǎo	V	to provide reference
10. 乐趣	lèqù	N	pleasure
11. 难过	nánguò	A	sad, upset
12. 院子	yuànzi	N	courtyard
13. 照顾	zhàogù	V	to look after
14. 关心	guānxīn	V	to care for
15. 美化	měihuà	V	to beautify
16. 心灵	xīnlíng	N	soul

注释　Notes

④ 弟子不必不如师，师不必贤于弟子。

"Disciples are not necessarily inferior to their teachers, while teachers are not necessarily wiser than their disciples."

This is a quotation from the essay *On Teachers* (《师说》) by Han Yu（韩愈，768—824），a famous writer of the Tang Dynasty.

⑤ 我已经把你们的名字写上了，请多提意见。

"I have already written your names on the books. Your suggestions will be highly appreciated."

When Chinese authors or artists present their books or other works as gifts to others, in addition to signing on the title page, they will also write the recipient's name and a request for comments and suggestions. For example, "马大为先生指正"（指正：zhǐzhèng, to make comments and suggestions）means "To Mr. Ma Dawei. Your suggestions will be highly appreciated."

二、练习　Exercises

练习 与运用　Drills and Practice 11

核心句 KEY SENTENCES

1. 墙上挂着中国字画。
2. 外边还整整齐齐地摆着这么多花儿。
3. 红红的花儿，真好看。
4. 这种花儿很好养。
5. 养花儿是不太难。
6. 工作累了的时候，我就把这些盆景修整修整。
7. 我哪儿是园艺师？这只是一点儿爱好。
8. 你还要更多地练习。

1. 熟读下列词组 Read the following phrases until you learn them by heart

（1）好养　好做　好学　好查　好找　好办　好写　好用　好骑　好搬

　　　不好复习　　　不好翻译　　　不好管理　　　不好修整　　　不好准备

（2）挂着很多图片　　　　住着两个留学生　　　　摆着一大盘糖

　　　戴着那条围巾　　　　站着一位服务员　　　　写着他的名字

　　　停着一辆汽车　　　　坐着一位书法家　　　　放着一套西服

　　　躺着一个小孩儿　　　穿着新的中式衣服

（3）大大的嘴　　　低低的声音　　　高高的大楼　　　远远的山

　　　漂漂亮亮的客厅　　　　干干净净的书房　　　　舒舒服服的卧室

（4）慢慢地走　　　轻轻地放　　　早早地出发　　　远远地看

　　　不高兴地说　　　非常客气地问　　　更多地练习　　　很好地休息

　　　整整齐齐地排队　　　高高兴兴地唱歌　　　安安静静地看书

　　　热热闹闹地过春节　　　辛辛苦苦地工作　　　认认真真地锻炼

（5）把这些刀叉洗洗　　　把礼物包一包　　　把这些汉字写一写

　　　把宿舍打扫打扫　　　　把这些盆景修整修整

　　　把学过的课文复习复习　　　把你做的练习检查检查

2. 句型替换 Pattern drills

（1）A：墙上 挂着 中国字画没有？

　　　B：墙上 挂着 中国字画呢。

本子上	写	他的名字
阳台上	放	很多盆花儿
桌子上	摆	一大盘糖
床旁边	放	一束花儿
咖啡馆前边	停	一辆汽车

（2）A：这个楼里人多吗?

　　　B：这个楼里住着二十个足球队员。

客厅	坐	四位画家
这辆公共汽车	站	很多乘客
那个房间	住	两个留学生
那个银行	排	很长的队

（3）A：他每天都练书法吗?

　　　B：他每天都认认真真地练书法。

姑娘们	唱歌	高高兴兴
小孩儿们	上课	安安静静
队员们	排队	整整齐齐
服务员	打扫房间	辛辛苦苦

（4）A：这个地方怎么样?

　　　B：有红红的花儿，真好看。

这个小区	有高高的大楼	很漂亮
那个公园	能看到远远的山	景色真美
这家咖啡馆	有轻轻的音乐	很安静
张教授的家	有干干净净的书房	很有特色

（5）A：应该把这些花儿浇一浇，对吗？

　　　B：对，我也是这样想的。咱们开始吧。

这些刀叉	洗
这个礼物	包
这些汉字	写
宿舍	扫

（6）A：昨天她下了课做什么了？

　　　B：昨天她下了课就去买花儿了。

换	钱	王府井买衣服
化	妆	听音乐会
参观	博物馆	访问张教授
浇	花儿	修整盆景

（7）A：这种花儿好养吗？

　　　B：这种花儿很好养。

这个菜	做	很好
这家医院	找	很好
汉字书法	学	不好
广州话	懂	不好

3. 课堂活动　Classroom activity

One student makes a sentence. Another uses "是" to emphasize and confirm this statement, and then uses "不过" to supplement it. For example,

A：外国人学汉字书法不容易。

B：外国人学汉字书法是不容易。不过，我看过很多留学生写的汉字，不比中国学生写的差。

4. 会话练习 Conversation practice

会话常用语 IDIOMATIC EXPRESSIONS IN CONVERSATION

人们常说 (People often say…)

我也是这样想的 (I think so, too.)

不知道行不行 (I do not know if it will be all right.)

请多提意见 (Your suggestions will be highly appreciated.)

【描述事物 Describing something】

（1）A：你去过陈老师家吗？

B：去过。她家客厅真大，也很漂亮。

A：客厅里有什么？

B：西边墙上挂着一幅油画，下边放着电视机（diànshìjī）。旁边的柜子（guìzi）里摆着很多外国的纪念品。东边放着大沙发（shāfā），沙发旁边还放着一盆君子兰。

（2）A：昨天晚上你看学校的时装（shízhuāng）表演了吗？

B：我看了，你觉得谁的表演最好？

A：我觉得林娜的表演很有特色。她身上穿着黑、白两种颜色的旗袍，戴着白的丝绸围巾，手里拿着黑皮包（píbāo），非常漂亮。她在台上走得也很优美。

B：林娜妆也化得很好看，大大的眼睛（yǎnjing），高高的鼻子（bízi），大大的嘴。我看她有希望赢。

【强调肯定 Emphasizing an affirmation】

A：今年的花儿没有去年开得好。

B：今年的花儿是没有去年开得好。可能你浇水浇多了。

A：我是浇得多了点儿。可是和别的花儿相比，君子兰不是开得很好吗？

【表示谦虚 Expressing modesty】

（1）A：我想问您一个书法的问题。

B：我对书法也了解得不多，咱们一起讨论（tǎolùn）讨论吧。

……

B：我的这些看法不一定都对，只能给你作参考（cānkǎo）。

A：您太谦虚了。您说得真好，对我有很大帮助。我看过您的很多书法作品，您真是一位书法家。

B：我哪儿是书法家？这只是一点儿爱好。

（2）A：我看了您写的书，我觉得非常好，我学到了很多东西。

B：哪里。那是我三年以前写的，很多看法不一定对。请多提意见。

5. 看图说话　Describe the following picture

（挂着　　摆着　　放着）

6. 交际练习 Communication exercises

(1) Do you agree that "disciples are not necessarily inferior to their teachers, while teachers are not necessarily wiser than their disciples"? Why or why not?

(2) How do you respond to other people's compliments?

After you speak, write down what you have said.

阅读与复述 Reading Comprehension and Paraphrasing

🎧12　老舍养花儿

　　我爱花儿，所以也爱养花儿。可是，我还不是园艺师，因为没有时间去提高养花儿技术。我只把养花儿看成生活中的一种乐趣 (lè-qù)。我养的花儿虽然不少，但是没有太名贵的花儿。我养的花儿开花儿了，我就高兴。名贵的花儿不好养，如果你看着一盆名贵的花儿得病了，心里是会很难过 (nánguò) 的。所以我的小院子 (yuànzi) 里整整齐齐地摆着那么多花儿，都是些好养的。当然，我还得天天照顾 (zhàogù) 它们，像好朋友一样地关心 (guānxīn) 它们，了解它们的生活情况。不这样，它们还是会死的。有它们的帮助，我也知道该怎么养花儿了。现在，我的小院子里，花儿越来越多，真让人高兴。

　　我身体不太好。花儿得到我的照顾，它们感谢不感谢我，我不知道。不过，我得感谢它们。我工作累了的时候，就到院子里去看看它们，给它们浇浇水，把那些盆景修整修整，然后再工作。我每天都要这样做，这是很好的休息，对身体很有好处。我觉得这比吃药还好。

　　开花儿了，朋友们来看我，我们一起去小院子里赏花儿。看着那些绿绿的叶子，红红的花儿，他们都称赞我养的花儿长得好！我心里特别高兴。我常把自己养的花儿当做礼物送给朋友，他们都很喜欢，还说，养花儿不但能美化 (měihuà) 生活，而且能美化人的心灵 (xīnlíng)。听了朋友们的话，我更觉得养花儿是一件很有乐趣的事儿了。

三、语法　Grammar

1　存现句（2）　Sentences indicating existence or emergence (2)

One kind of sentence that indicates the existence and location (of somebody or something) was introduced in Lesson 21. Here is another kind of sentence. Its subject is a noun or phrase of location; its predicate is "V+着"; and its object is somebody or something that exists.

Its negative form is "没有＋V＋着"，while its affirmative-negative form is "V＋着＋没有".

S (PW) + V + 着 + Num–MP + O (somebody or something that exists)

Subject (PW)	Predicate			
	V	着	Num–MP	O (somebody or something that exists)
墙上	挂	着		中国字画没有？
外边	摆	着	两盆	花儿。
桌子上	没（有）放	着	一台	电脑。
房间里	站	着	很多	服务员。
客厅里	坐	着	一位	书法家。

Notes:

❶ The prepositions such as "在" and "从" are not placed in front of the subject.

❷ The adverbs "在" and "正在" cannot be placed in front of the verbs, so one cannot say: "墙上正在挂着中国字画。"

❸ The object is usually preceded by a numeral-measure phrase or another phrase as its attributive.

2　形容词重叠　Reduplication of an adjective

Adjectives describing characteristics or qualities can usually be reduplicated. The reduplicative form of a monosyllabic adjective is "AA". For example, 红红，绿绿 and 长长. The reduplicative form of a disyllabic adjective is "AABB". For example, 整整齐齐，干干净净 and 漂漂亮亮. An adjective is often reduplicated to indicate a higher degree of a certain quality than its non-reduplicative counterpart, used to describe something and sometimes, to express the speaker's fondness or praise. For example，红红的花儿 and 长长的绿叶。

3 结构助词"地" The structural particle "地"

When a reduplicated adjective or an adjectival phrase functions as an adverbial modifier, the structural particle "地" is usually added. For example,

> 这里边是盘子，请你轻轻地放。
>
> 书架上整整齐齐地摆着很多古书。
>
> 多看中文电视就能更快地提高汉语水平。

4 "把"字句（4） The "把" sentence (4)

A reduplicated verb can also be used in the "把" sentence. In this kind of "把" sentence, the reduplicated verb may not be followed by other elements. For example,

$$S + 把 + O_把 + V V$$

Subject	Predicate		
	把	O_把	V V
你	把 请把	这些盆景 那些水果	修整修整吧。 洗一洗。

四、字与词 Chinese Characters and Words

构词法（3）：补充式

Word formation method (3): Verb-complement compound words

This kind of compound word is composed of a verb and a complement, e.g. "提 + 高"→ "提高". The second character complements the first one. For example, "打开, 得到, 记得, 站住".

Chinese Calligraphy

Chinese calligraphy is a unique visual art based on Chinese characters. It boasts a long history and a good variety of styles, which are divided into the seal script, official script, cursive script, running script and regular script in general terms.

The seal script was used before the Han Dynasty (206 B.C.–220 A.D.). Since the Han Dynasty, it has been predominantly used in seals for its smooth and elegant looking.

The official script was created during the Qin and Han dynasties (221 B.C.–220 A.D.). In the official script, the line characteristic of the seal script was replaced by the dot, endowing Chinese characters distinct strokes. The Han Dynasty witnessed the maturity of the official script.

The regular script took shape later than the official script and has become the standard style of handwriting since the Sui and Tang dynasties (581–907) up to date. A complete set of stroke shapes was formed in the regular script.

The cursive script that emerged in the Han Dynasty is another common script in addition to the three scripts mentioned above. It is written in a scrawly way at a rapid speed. In the later Eastern Han Dynasty (25–220), a new style called the running script came into being. It is subject to no strict writing rules. The neatly and carefully written running characters look similar to the regular script, while those hastily written ones are more like the cursive script. Written at a faster speed than the regular script and being less illegible than the cursive script, the running script is much loved by Chinese people. Nowadays, it is the most frequently used script in the daily life of Chinese people and in their work and study.

In the Chinese history, there were a lot of outstanding calligraphers, the most famous one being Wang Xizhi of the Eastern Jin Dynasty (317–420). As a master in a number of scripts such as the official, the regular, the cursive and the running, Wang Xizhi learned the skills from many others and created his own style, being acknowledged as the Sage of Calligraphy by later generations.

In September 2009, Chinese calligraphy was inscribed on the Representative List of the Intangible Cultural Heritage of Humanity.

第三十课

Lesson 30

他们是练太极剑的

They are practicing taiji sword.

After supper, Ding Libo, Ma Dawei and Song Hua take a walk on the street in a residential area in Beijing. They find that Beijing residents have their own special recreational activities...

一、课文　Text

🎧 13 （一）

丁力波：现在八点半了，街上还这么热闹！

宋　华：这儿的人吃完晚饭都喜欢出来活动活动。你看，人们又唱又
　　　　跳，玩儿得真高兴。

马大为：那儿来了很多人，一边跳舞，一边
　　　　还敲锣打鼓。他们在跳什么舞？

> 描述事物
> **Describing something**

宋　华：他们在扭秧歌呢。

马大为：扭秧歌？我听说过。

宋　华：这是中国北方的一种民间舞蹈，叫做秧歌舞。秧歌舞的动作
　　　　又简单又好看，小孩儿、大姑娘、小伙子、老人都可以跳。

对老人来说，现在扭秧歌已经是一种锻炼身体的活动了。他们很喜欢扭，常常扭得全身出汗。

马大为：我看，这种舞很好跳，我也能很快学会。我跟他们一起扭，可以吗？

宋　华：当然可以。

马大为：不行，我还得先把动作练一练，要不，大家就都看我一个人扭了。① 前边又走过来了不少老人，他们手里都拿着什么？

宋　华：他们是练太极剑的，手里拿的是剑。太极剑也是中国武术的一种，练太极剑可以很好地锻炼身体。我妈妈以前常常生病，不能工作。后来，她就练太极剑。② 练了两年，她身体好了，现在可以上班了。力波，你不是每天早上都学太极拳吗？现在你学得怎么样了？

表示变化
Indicating a change

丁力波：现在我已经会打太极拳了。最近，又开始学太极剑。我觉得打太极拳、练太极剑对身体是很好。

宋　华：太极剑的动作非常优美，练太极剑就没有扭秧歌那么容易了。

马大为：你们看，街心花园那儿围着很多人。那儿安静得没有一点儿声音，他们在做什么呢？咱们过去看看。

生词 New Words

1. 太极剑	tàijíjiàn	N	*taiji* sword (a kind of traditional Chinese swordplay)　练太极剑
剑	jiàn	N	sword　拿着一把剑
2. 街	jiē	N	street　街上，大街，一条街
3. 活动	huódòng	V/N	to exercise; activity　出来活动，活动活动；有什么活动，一种锻炼身体的活动
4. 跳	tiào	V	to jump, to leap　又唱又跳，跳起来
5. 跳舞	tiàowǔ	VO	to dance　喜欢跳舞，跳什么舞，跳古典舞
舞	wǔ	N	dance
6. 敲锣打鼓	qiāo luó dǎ gǔ	IE	to beat drums and gongs
敲	qiāo	V	to beat, to knock (at/on sth.)　敲门
锣	luó	N	gong
*打	dǎ	V	to beat
鼓	gǔ	N	drum
7. 扭秧歌	niǔ yāngge	V O	to do the *yangge* dance
扭	niǔ	V	to twist, to turn
秧歌	yāngge	N	*yangge* dance
8. 民间	mínjiān	N	folk　民间音乐，民间故事，民间艺术，跳民间舞
9. 舞蹈	wǔdǎo	N	dance　舞蹈专业，舞蹈学院，舞蹈艺术，民间舞蹈
10. 叫做	jiàozuò	V	to be called　叫做秧歌舞，叫做入乡随俗
11. 动作	dòngzuò	N	movement, action　舞蹈动作，练练动作，太极剑的动作
12. 简单	jiǎndān	A	simple　简单的动作，简单的问题，简单的事儿，简单介绍，简单回答

13.	老人	lǎorén	N	senior citizen, elderly man or woman　尊重老人，帮助老人
14.	出汗	chū hàn	V O	to sweat　头上出汗，扭得全身出汗，热得出汗，出了很多汗
15.	要不	yàobù	Conj	otherwise, or else
16.	武术	wǔshù	N	martial arts　练武术，中国武术，武术比赛
17.	生病	shēngbìng	VO	to fall ill　常常生病，生病的时候
	病	bìng	V/N	to fall ill; disease　病了，病得很重；小病，大病，病好了，一种病
18.	后来	hòulái	N	afterwards, later　后来怎么样，后来呢
19.	上班	shàngbān	VO	to go to work　在邮局上班，上班时间
20.	早上	zǎoshang	N	(early) morning　每天早上，早上好
21.	最近	zuìjìn	N	recently　最近一个月，最近三天
22.	街心花园	jiēxīn huāyuán		street garden
*23.	围	wéi	V	to surround　围着他，围着很多人，围着看

注释　Notes

① 我还得先把动作练一练，要不，大家就都看我一个人扭了。

　　"I have to practice the basic movements first. Otherwise, everybody will just be watching me dancing."

　　"要不" means "如果不" ("otherwise" or "if not"). It is used between two clauses or sentences to introduce the result or conclusion that is derived from the assumption or expectation contrary to the first sentence. For example,

　　　　你去参加她的生日聚会吧，要不，她会不高兴的。

② 后来，她就练太极剑。

　　"Later, she practiced *taiji* sword."

　　"后来" refers to a time after a certain period in the past. For example,

他去年五月去过一次，后来没有再去过。

Note: The differences between 后来 and 以后：(a) 以后 can refer to a time either in the past or future, while 后来 refers only to a time in the past. (b) 以后 can be used either alone or with other words; for example, 下课以后 . However, 后来 can only be used by itself. Thus, one cannot say: 下课后来 .

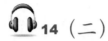 14 （二）

丁力波：他们在下棋呢。宋华，你喜欢下棋吗？

宋　华：喜欢。我也喜欢看别人下棋。我觉得看别人下比自己下更有意思。有的时候我看得忘了吃饭。

马大为：所以那些站在旁边的人也是在看下棋？

宋　华：是啊，常常两个人下棋，很多人围着看。看的人和下的人也可能互相不认识。

马大为：这很有意思。

丁力波： 东边的立交桥下还有很多人呢。你听见了吗？那是唱京剧的。

马大为： 京剧团怎么到这儿来唱呢？

宋　华： 他们不是京剧团的，他们是这个小区的京剧爱好者，也都是些老人。以前他们工作的时候，忙得没有时间唱。现在他们人退休了，休闲的

时间也多了，晚上就来这儿高高兴兴地唱一唱。因为爱好一样，不认识的人也都成了朋友。一般说来，到这儿来唱的人水平都还可以，喜欢听京剧的就围过来听。他们听得高兴的时候，也可以叫"好"，这也是他们的一种休闲方式。

马大为： 真有意思。我发现这里的老人休闲活动有很多特点。简单地说，第一，他们非常注意锻炼身体；第二，最重要的是，他们喜欢很多人在一起活动；第三，有的人做，有的人看，可能互相不认识，可是大家都玩儿得很高兴。

> 总结概括
> **Making a summary**

宋　华： 你说得很对。当然，这里的老人休闲方式还很多。早上有做操的，有跑步的，有爬山的，有游泳的，也有带着自己的小狗散步的，还有在家练书法的、养花儿的。③

马大为：年轻人呢？

宋　华：年轻人的休闲活动就更多了。你看，街对面的网吧门口进进

出出的都是年轻人，④旁边的舞厅里又出来了两个小伙子。

生词 New Words

1.	下棋	xiàqí	VO	to play chess　看别人下棋，喜欢下棋，跟朋友下棋，下一盘棋
2.	立交桥	lìjiāoqiáo	N	overpass　立交桥下，上立交桥，下立交桥
	桥	qiáo	N	bridge
3.	听见	tīngjiàn	VC	to hear　听见声音，没有听见
4.	爱好者	àihàozhě	N	lover (of art, sports, etc.), enthusiast　京剧爱好者，书法爱好者
5.	退休	tuìxiū	V	to retire　退休以后，退休教师，退休老人
6.	休闲	xiūxián	V	to have leisure　休闲时间，休闲活动
7.	方式	fāngshì	N	way　休闲方式，活动方式，生活方式
8.	做操	zuòcāo	VO	to do gymnastics
9.	跑步	pǎobù	VO	to jog
10.	对面	duìmiàn	N	opposite side　街对面，大楼对面
11.	网吧	wǎngbā	N	Internet cafe, cybercafe　街对面的网吧，一个网吧
12.	门口	ménkǒu	N	doorway　网吧门口，学校门口，家门口
13.	舞厅	wǔtīng	N	ballroom　旁边的舞厅，去舞厅跳舞

补充生词 Supplementary Words

1. 违反	wéifǎn	V	to violate
2. 长寿	chángshòu	A	longevity
3. 公里	gōnglǐ	M	kilometer
4. 调查	diàochá	V	to investigate
5. 组	zǔ	M	set, series, group
6. 心脏	xīnzàng	N	heart
7. 秘诀	mìjué	N	secret (of success)
8. 在于	zàiyú	V	to depend on, to rely on
9. 运动	yùndòng	V/N	to do physical exercise; sports
10. 奥林匹克	Àolínpǐkè	PN	the Olympics
11. 故乡	gùxiāng	N	hometown
12. 流传	liúchuán	V	to spread
13. 健康	jiànkāng	A	healthy
14. 聪明	cōngming	A	intelligent, clever

注释 Notes

③ 早上有做操的，有跑步的，有爬山的，有游泳的，也有带着自己的小狗散步的，还有在家练书法的、养花儿的。

"In the morning, some people do gymnastics, some jog, some climb hills, and some swim. There are also people who take their dogs for a walk, or stay at home practicing calligraphy or growing flowers."

Two or more of the structure "有+VP+的" may be used to express enumeration.

④ 街对面的网吧门口进进出出的都是年轻人。

"All those (who are) going in and out of that Internet bar across the street are young people."

二、练习　Exercises

练习 与运用　**Drills and Practice** 15

核心句 KEY SENTENCES

1. 现在八点半了。
2. 他们玩儿得真高兴。
3. 秧歌舞的动作又简单又好看。
4. 我还得先把动作练一练，要不，大家就都看我一个人扭了。
5. 前边走过来了不少老人。
6. 我妈妈以前常常生病，不能工作。后来，她就练太极剑。
7. 她身体好了，现在可以上班了。
8. 以前他们忙得没有时间唱。
9. 舞厅里出来了两个小伙子。

1. 熟读下列词组 Read the following phrases until you learn them by heart

（1）来了两个新同学　　开来了一辆公共汽车　　下去了很多大学生
　　死了一只小狗　　　走过来了不少年轻人

（2）玩儿得很高兴　　　病得不能起床　　　　热得全身出汗
　　高兴得跳起来了　　累得不想说话

（3）会下棋了　　会扭秧歌了　　会唱京剧了　　会开汽车了
　　可以上班了　　该出发了　　　能上学了　　　愿意养花儿了

（4）又唱歌又跳舞　　又简单又好看　　又工作又学习
　　又洗衣又做饭　　又年轻又漂亮　　又干净又安静

2. 句型替换　Pattern drills

（1）前边 走过来了不少老人。

楼下	来	两个新同学
南边	开来	一辆公共汽车
火车上	下去	很多大学生
外婆家	死	一只小狗
对面	走过来	不少年轻人

（2）以前他会不会 打太极拳?
　　以前他不会 打太极拳。
　　现在呢?
　　现在他已经会 打太极拳了。

会	下棋
会	扭秧歌
会	开汽车
能	上班
愿意	养花儿

（3）他们 玩儿得怎么样?
　　他们 玩儿得真高兴。

大家	唱	嗓子疼
那位老人	病	不能起床
小伙子	跳舞跳	全身出汗
京剧爱好者	听京剧听	忘了吃饭

（4）他忙不忙?
　　他很忙, 忙得没有时间唱京剧。

高兴	跳起来了
累	不想说话
热	全身出汗
疼	躺在床上

（5）秧歌舞的动作 简单吗？

秧歌舞的动作 又简单又好看。

他姐姐	工作	又工作又学习
这书房	干净	又干净又安静
她丈夫	做饭	又做饭又洗衣服
他妻子	漂亮	又漂亮又年轻

（6）我还得先把动作练一练，要不，大家就都看我一个人扭了。

把去农村的路问清楚	我们又该找错地方了
打电话告诉她	她不会在家等我们
把课文念一念	上课的时候我又会念得很不流利了
了解一下那儿的风俗	我不知道该怎么做

3. 课堂活动 Classroom activities

(1) One student makes a sentence using the words learned in this lesson, and another student uses "后来" to continue the conversation. For example,

A：我来北京以后常常去网吧。

B：后来在那儿认识了一个中国朋友。

(2) One student makes a sentence using the words learned in this lesson, and another student uses "要不" to make an inference. For example,

A：我们现在应该学点儿武术。

B：要不，以后就没有这么方便了。

4. 会话练习 Conversation practice

> **会话常用语** *IDIOMATIC EXPRESSIONS IN CONVERSATION*
>
> 当然可以 (Of course.)
>
> 要不 (Otherwise, ...)
>
> 一般说来 (Generally speaking, ...)
>
> 简单地说 (In a word, ...)
>
> 最重要的是 (The most important thing is...)

【表示变化　Indicating a change】

A：你最近听到王文的消息了吗? 他在家里休息得怎么样?

B：他已经从家里回来了。现在他身体好了，每天能正常学习了。

A：他两个月不在学校，现在学习怎么样?

B：他学习进步得也很快。他的变化真大。

【总结概括　Making a summary】

A：不同的地方有不同的风俗习惯，你觉得我们应该怎样做?

B：简单地说，我觉得"入乡随俗"是对的。怎样"入乡随俗"呢?
第一，要尊重别人的风俗习惯，也就是尊重别人的文化; 第二，
如果你喜欢这种风俗习惯，你也可以这样做。

A：如果我不愿意这样做呢?

B：你当然可以不做，但是你也应该注意：不要违反（wéifǎn）别人的风
俗习惯。

A：你说得很对。最重要的是尊重别人。

5. 看图说话　Describe the following picture

金源商场

（坐着　放着　开着　开过来　开走　走出来　走进去）

6. 交际练习　Communication exercises

(1) What changes have occurred to you, or to one of your friends, classmates, teachers recently? Describe them.

(2) Discuss how to study Chinese characters, memorize new words, or practice spoken Chinese based on your experience.

After you speak, write down what you have said.

阅读与复述 Reading Comprehension and Paraphrasing

16　走路和长寿（chángshòu）

　　人们常说："饭后百步走，活到九十九。"走路是最方便的活动方式，也是老年人最好的锻炼。怎么走呢？医生建议老年人每天用三十分钟的时间，走三公里（gōnglǐ）的路，每个星期最少走五次。当然，用多少时间，走多少路，那还得看自己的身体情况。身体好的，可以多走一些；身体差的，也可以少走一些。只要每天都走走，对身体一定有好处。

一位医生调查（diàochá）了两组（zǔ）老人。一组是每天走一个小时；一组是每天很少走路。后来他发现每天走路的人长寿，得心脏（xīnzàng）病的少。

一个记者访问了一位95岁的老人。他问老人，健康长寿的秘诀（mìjué）是什么？老人笑着说："我哪有什么秘诀？人们常说，生命在于（zàiyú）运动（yùndòng）。年轻人要运动，老年人更要常运动。"记者又问他："您喜欢什么运动？"老人说："我最大的爱好就是走路，每天最少走一个小时的路。早上起床以后就到公园里去走一走，要走得全身都热了，但是不要热得全身出汗。走完了一小时的路，才回家吃饭、看书、看报、看电视。"老人觉得，每天走路，又简单又方便。如果有可能，再去爬爬山，那就更好了。记者想，"走路"可能就是这位老人的长寿秘诀吧。

奥林匹克（Àolínpǐkè）运动的故乡（gùxiāng）流传（liúchuán）着这样的几句话："你想变得健康（jiànkāng）吗？你就跑步吧。你想变得聪明（cōngming）吗？你就跑步吧。你想变得漂亮吗？你就跑步吧。"对老年人，我们也可以这样说："你想健康吗？你就走路吧。你想长寿吗？你就走路吧。"

三、语法　Grammar

1 存现句（3）　Sentences indicating existence or emergence (3)

　　The following sentence pattern is commonly used to describe the appearance or disappearance of somebody or something at some place.

S (PW) + V + Pt or Complement + Num-MP+ O

(somebody or something that appears or disappears)

Subject (PW)	Predicate			
	V	Pt or Complement	Num-MP	O (somebody or something that appears or disappears)
那儿	来	了	很多	人。
前边	走	过来	不少	老人。
他们家	死	了	一盆	花儿。
立交桥下	开	过去	五辆	车。
宿舍门口	丢	了	一辆	自行车。

Notes:

❶ The subject of this type of sentence is a word or phrase indicating location. The prepositions such as "在" and "从" cannot be inserted before the subject.

❷ The predicate of this type of sentence is an intransitive verb that usually indicates the change of somebody or something in position. For example, "走，跑，来，丢，生，死".

❸ The verb of this type of sentence is commonly followed by the aspect particle "了" or a complement.

❹ The object of this type of sentence is not specified. Thus, one cannot say: "前边走来了马大为." There is usually a numeral-measure phrase or another attributive in front of the object.

2 "了" 表示情况的变化 (2)

"了" indicating a change in circumstances (2)

A sentence with a noun phrase, a subject-predicate phrase, or an optative verb as the predicate can be followed by "了" at the end of the sentence to indicate a change in circumstances or emergence of some new situation. This kind of sentence functions as a reminder or is used to attract people's attention. For example,

A: 现在几点了?

B: 现在八点半了。

A：他几岁了？

B：他八岁了。

我妈妈身体好了，现在可以上班了。

现在他们人退休了，休闲的时间也多了。

丁力波会打太极拳了。

现在可以进来了。

The structure "……了+没有" can be used as the interrogative form of this type of sentence. For example,

她身体好了没有？

3 情态补语（2）　Modal complement (2)

Besides describing or commenting on a movement or an action itself, a modal complement is often used to describe the mood or state of the subject (somebody or something) that is caused by a movement or an action. For example,

他们玩儿得很高兴。

水果洗得干干净净的。

Besides an adjectival phrase, a verbal phrase, subject-predicate phrase and other complement can also serve as a modal complement. For example,

那儿安静得没有一点儿声音。(verbal phrase)

他们下棋下得忘了吃饭。

他们忙得没有时间唱京剧。

他们扭得全身出汗。(subject-predicate phrase)

他高兴得跳起来了。(directional complement)

我累得躺在床上。(resultative complement)

4 又……又……　　The construction "又……又……"

"又"(3) is followed by a verbal/adjectival word or phrase, indicating that several actions, features or states occur or exist at the same time. For example,

他们又唱又跳。

那些人又说又笑，真高兴。

秧歌舞的动作又简单又好看。

这个姑娘又年轻又漂亮。

他在北京又工作又上学。

四、字与词　Chinese Characters and Words

构词法（4）：动宾式

Word formation method (4): Verb-object compound words

The first character dominates the meaning of the second one, e.g. "结+果→结果". Other examples include,

| 说话 | 食物 | 聊天儿 | 照相 | 送礼 | 下棋 | 结业 | 吃饭 | 放心 | 放假 |
| 挂号 | 烤鸭 | 排队 | 起床 | 散步 | 跳舞 | 唱歌 | 开车 | 看病 | 罚款 |

Chinese Martial Arts

As an important part of traditional Chinese culture and China's national sports, martial arts have been practiced by Chinese people for improving their health and self-defense for thousands of years. Chinese martial arts, also called "kung fu", are one of the quintessential specialties of China.

Chinese martial arts include various skills and strategies of striking with fists, wrestling, attacking and defending, and fighting with weapons. The major established series of skills and tricks include boxing and the proper use of sabers, spears, swords and sticks. There are numerous schools of Chinese martial arts. Statistics show that for boxing alone, there are more than 300 schools which have a known history, a distinct style and a self-independent system. The martial arts familiar to people today include Shaolin boxing, *taijiquan* (Chinese shadow boxing) and *qigong* (a system of deep breathing exercises), etc.

The reason for the variety of schools lies in the differences between southern and northern China in terms of geographic and climatic conditions and statures of people. Generally speaking, people in northern China are taller and bigger and the weather there is much colder. As a result, boxing in northern China is full of momentum and strength. And boxing in southern China, where the climate is humid and water is abundant and people are smaller and shorter in stature, seems more smooth and elegant.

What's embodied in Chinese martial arts is the philosophical spirit of Chinese people. The practitioners of martial arts attach great importance to "the virtues of martial arts". They advocate peace and building up a good physique, and believe that one is not supposed to initiate fights against other people and should shoulder social responsibilities. The first person that brought Chinese martial arts to the world stage was Bruce Lee, who was hailed as the King of Kung Fu and the Sage of Martial Arts. Credits should also be given to other kung fu movie stars like Jackie Chan and Jet Lee and many other cultural ambassadors for their efforts in presenting the charm of Chinese martial arts to the world. Oweing to them, Chinese kung fu have now become well-known to people all over the world.

第三十一课
Lesson
31

中国人叫它 "母亲河"

Chinese people refer to it as "the Mother River".

Lin Na and Ding Libo want to participate in the "China Expert Knowledge Contest". They ask Song Hua to help them prepare. Read the following conversation to see how they are getting ready for the contest.

一、课文 Text

🎧 17 （一）

林 娜：宋华，学校让我和力波参加"中国通知识大赛"。我们虽然

来中国一年多了，可是对中国的地理知识还了解得不太多。

现在只有一个多月的时间准备了，我们着急得吃不下饭，睡

不好觉。①

宋 华：一共有多少人参加这次比赛？

丁力波：听说有二十几个人。

宋 华：不用着急。你们只要认真准备，

就一定会得到好的成绩。

表示鼓励
Giving an encouragement

丁力波: 你帮我们准备一下，好吗？

宋　华: 好啊。我先问你们一个问题：中国很大，有多大呢？

丁力波: 中国的国土面积有九百六十万平方公里，[②]从东到西，有五千二百多公里；从南到北，有五千五百多公里，是世界第三大国家。

> **询问事物的性状**
> **Asking about the property or state of something**

林　娜: 对。俄罗斯最大。中国比美国大一点儿，比加拿大小一点儿。

宋　华: 中国的人口有多少？

丁力波: 中国的人口，包括大陆、台湾、香港和澳门，一共有十三亿多。[③]中国是世界上人口最多的国家。

宋　华: 回答正确。下一个问题：世界上最高的地方在哪儿？

林　娜: 在中国的西藏。

宋　华: 世界上最高的山峰叫什么？它有多高？

丁力波: 世界上最高的山峰叫珠穆朗玛峰，它有8800多米高。

宋　华: 中国最长的河是不是黄河？

林　娜: 不是。中国第一大河是长江，有6300多公里长。它也是世界第三大河。黄河是中国第二大河，有5400多公里长。

宋　华: 中国人为什么叫黄河"母亲河"？

丁力波: 黄河是中华民族的摇篮，所以中国人叫它"母亲河"。[④]

生词 New Words

1. 母亲	mǔqīn	N	mother	我母亲
母	mǔ		mother	
2. 河	hé	N	river	小河，大河，第一大河，母亲河，一条河
3. 知识	zhīshi	N	knowledge	文化知识，历史知识，音乐知识，知识比赛，知识大赛
4. 地理	dìlǐ	N	geography	中国地理，中国的地理知识
5. 只要	zhǐyào	Conj	as long as	
6. 成绩	chéngjì	N	test result	学习成绩，考试成绩，比赛成绩，好的成绩
7. 国土	guótǔ	N	land	中国的国土，国土面积
8. 面积	miànjī	N	area	中国的面积，北京的面积
9. 万	wàn	Nu	ten thousand	一万，十万，一百万，一千万
10. 平方公里	píngfāng gōnglǐ	M	square kilometer	九百六十万平方公里
平方	píngfāng	M	square	平方米
公里	gōnglǐ	M	kilometer	五千五百多公里，六千三百多公里长，五千四百多公里长
11. 世界	shìjiè	N	world	世界上，全世界，世界有名
12. 人口	rénkǒu	N	population	中国人口，有多少人口，人口最多的国家
13. 包括	bāokuò	V	to include	包括小孩儿，包括郊区
14. 亿	yì	Nu	a hundred million	十三亿七千万，十三亿人口
15. 正确	zhèngquè	A	correct	正确的回答，正确的看法，正确的意见，正确的方式
16. 山峰	shānfēng	N	peak	最高的山峰

17.	米	mǐ	M	meter	八千八百多米高，一米八，一米七五
18.	摇篮	yáolán	N	cradle	小孩儿的摇篮，民族的摇篮
19.	俄罗斯	Éluósī	PN	Russia	
20.	大陆	Dàlù	PN	the mainland (of China)	
21.	台湾	Táiwān	PN	Taiwan	
22.	香港	Xiānggǎng	PN	Hong Kong	
23.	澳门	Àomén	PN	Macao	
24.	西藏	Xīzàng	PN	Tibet	
25.	珠穆朗玛峰	Zhūmùlǎngmǎ Fēng	PN	Mount Qomolangma (known in the West as Mount Everest)	
26.	黄河	Huáng Hé	PN	the Yellow River	
27.	长江	Cháng Jiāng	PN	the Changjiang River (or Yangtze River)	
28.	中华	Zhōnghuá	PN	China	

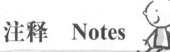

注释　Notes

① 我们着急得吃不下饭，睡不好觉。

"We are too worried to eat or sleep well."

② 中国的国土面积有九百六十万平方公里。

"China has a land area of 9.6 million square kilometers."

The construction "有+Num-MP（+A）" is employed to indicate the quantity that something has reached in terms of a property. The adjective in the construction that indicates the property is usually "大", "高", "长" or "重", etc. The interrogative form of this construction is "有+多+A". For example,

A：香港的面积有多大？　　　B：香港的面积有1100多平方公里。

A：珠穆朗玛峰有多高？　　　B：珠穆朗玛峰有8800多米高。

A：长江有多长？　　　　　　B：长江有6300多公里长。

A：这些苹果有多重？　　　　B：这些苹果有5斤多重。

A：他有多大（岁数）？　　　B：他有三十多岁。

A：他有多高？　　　　　　　B：他有一米八五。

"没（有）" is used to negate this construction. For example,

他没有三十岁。

他没有一米八五。

③ 中国的人口，包括大陆、台湾、香港和澳门，一共有十三亿多。

"The population of China, including the mainland, Taiwan, Hong Kong and Macao, amounts to more than 1.3 billion."

The verb "包括" means "to include" (some or all parts of something), and its negative form is "不包括". For example,

他每天在外边工作的时间，包括坐公共汽车，一共有十个小时。

我们系的学生，不包括旁听生（pángtīngshēng, auditor），有四百五十人。

④ 黄河是中华民族的摇篮，所以中国人叫它"母亲河"。

"The Yellow River is the cradle of Chinese nation. Therefore, the Chinese people refer to it as 'the Mother River'."

In ancient times, "中华" was referred to the Yellow River Valley, where the Han people, the largest ethnic group in China, firstly emerged. Later, it stood for China, and "中华民族" is now the general term for the 56 ethnic groups of China.

Such verbs as "叫" and "称" can take double objects to form the construction "叫(称)+O_1+O_2".

林娜叫丁力波"老画家"。

你可以叫出租汽车司机"师傅"。

大家称张教授园艺师。

🎧 18 （二）

宋　华：大为，刚才有人给你打电话了。

马大为：那可能是我的一个朋友打来的。要放长假了，有几个朋友想去旅游，可是还没有决定去哪儿。

宋　华：中国的名胜古迹太多了，有名的少说也有五六百个。⑤ 只要你喜欢旅游，每个假期都有地方去。

马大为：先去哪儿呢？我已经去过两三个地方了，有海南岛、西安，

　　　　对了，还有泰山。

宋　华：你喜欢游名胜古迹，还是喜欢看自然景色？

马大为：都喜欢。我特别喜欢爬山，爬又高又美的山。

宋　华：好啊。去爬珠穆朗玛峰吧，那是全世界最高的山。

马大为：那座山高了点儿，我的身体差了点儿，时间也少了点儿。

宋　华：黄山你还没有去过吧？

马大为：还没去过。黄山怎么样？

宋　华：那儿的景色是世界有名的。早
在1200多年以前，黄山就已经是
中国的名胜了。⑥ 你在那儿可以
看到，从早到晚景色在不停地
变化着。而且不同的人看，感
觉也不一样。它最美的景色是

白云、松树和山峰。你从山上往下看，

白云就像大海一样，⑦ 人们叫它“云

描写景色
Describing scenery

海”。黄山的松树和山峰也都很有特色。很多山峰样子都非
常奇怪，所以叫做“奇峰”，松树就长在这些奇峰上。云海、
松树和奇峰在一起真是美极了！不但中国人喜欢游黄山，而
且外国朋友也常去那儿。

马大为：黄山有一棵树叫做"迎客松"吧？

宋　华：对！那棵古松有1000多岁了，它每天都在热情地欢迎游黄山的朋友们。

马大为：好，下星期我就去黄山旅游。

生词 New Words

1. 旅游	lǚyóu	V	to tour	去旅游，去西安旅游
游	yóu	V	to travel, to tour	游泰山，游海南岛
2. 名胜古迹	míngshèng gǔjì	IE	scenic spots and historical sites	游名胜古迹，名胜古迹很多
名胜	míngshèng	N	scenic spots	
古迹	gǔjì	N	historical sites	
3. 自然	zìrán	N/A	nature; natural	自然景色；声调很自然，说得很自然
4. 感觉	gǎnjué	N/V	feeling; to feel	我的感觉；感觉不一样
5. 云	yún	N	cloud	白云
6. 松树	sōngshù	N	pine (tree)	
树	shù	N	tree	
7. 海	hǎi	N	sea	大海，像大海一样
8. 奇怪	qíguài	A	strange, odd	奇怪的山峰，奇怪的样子
9. 棵	kē	M	a measure word for plants	一棵树，一棵菜
10. 黄山	Huáng Shān	PN	Mt. Huang	
11. 迎客松	Yíngkèsōng	PN	Welcoming Pine (on Mt. Huang)	

补充生词 Supplementary Words

1.	诗人	shīrén	N	poet
2.	南水北调	nán shuǐ běi diào	IE	to divert water from the south to the north
3.	运河	yùnhé	N	canal
4.	杭州	Hángzhōu	PN	Hangzhou (a city in China)
5.	工程	gōngchéng	N	project
6.	挖	wā	V	to dig
7.	隋炀帝	Suí Yángdì	PN	Emperor Suiyangdi (569~618, an emperor of the Sui Dynasty)
8.	江南	Jiāngnán	PN	areas south of the Changjiang River
9.	柳树	liǔshù	N	willow
10.	扬州	Yángzhōu	PN	Yangzhou (a city in China)
11.	汇合	huìhé	V	to converge
12.	段	duàn	M	*a measure word used of a section of something long*
13.	通航	tōngháng	V	to be open to air traffic or navigation
14.	研究	yánjiū	V	to study, to research
15.	引	yǐn	V	to divert, to lead
16.	改善	gǎishàn	V	to improve

注释　Notes

⑤ 有名的少说也有五六百个。

"There are five to six hundred famous ones at least."

The meaning of "少说" is "at least". For example,

今天来的人很多，少说也有七八百人。

这是一棵老树，少说也有六百年了。

⑥ 早在1200多年以前，黄山就已经是中国的名胜了。

"As early as over 1,200 years ago, Mt. Huang was already a famous scenic spot in China."

"早在……以前" means "as early as". For example, 早在一个月前，早在1950年.

⑦ 白云就像大海一样。

"The white clouds look just like the vast sea."

"像" is a preposition in this sentence. "像+NP+一样" is used in almost the same way as "跟+NP+一样". For example, instead of "白云就像大海一样", one can say, "白云就跟大海一样".

二、练习　Exercises

练习 与运用　**Drills and Practice** 19

核心句 KEY SENTENCES

1. 听说有二十几个人参加比赛。
2. 你们只要认真准备，就一定会得到好的成绩。
3. 中国的国土面积有九百六十万平方公里。
4. 珠穆朗玛峰有8800多米高。
5. 中国人叫它"母亲河"。
6. 刚才有人给你打电话了。
7. 我已经去过两三个地方了。
8. 黄山有一棵树叫做"迎客松"吧?

1. 熟读下列词组　Read the following phrases until you learn them by heart

（1）几件事儿　　十几盆君子兰　　几十匹马　　三十几位老师

　　几百块钱　　十多斤水果　　二十多岁　　三十多瓶啤酒

　　二百多位书法家　　一千多块钱　　一斤多点心

　　五米多布　　两个多小时　　三个多星期　　七个多月

　　两三幅字画　　三四部电影　　一二十种月饼

　　五六十篇文章　　七八百辆汽车

（2）五万七千五百六十六公里（57566公里）

三十四万二千多公里（342000多公里）

五百万零九十五平方米（5000095平方米）

九百六十万平方公里（9600000平方公里）

十三亿七千万人（1370000000人）

（3）有人敲门　　有人找你　　有人给你打电话

有一个姑娘很漂亮　　　　有一位诗人叫李白

2. 句型替换　Pattern drills

（1）A：珠穆朗玛峰有多高?

　　B：珠穆朗玛峰有8800多米高。

中国的人口	多少	1300000000多
上海的人口	多少	23000000多
中国的国土面积	多大	9600000平方公里
北京的面积	多大	16400多平方公里
这条河	多长	5400多公里长

（2）A：这座桥有没有50米 长?

　　B：这座桥没有50米 长，只有40多米。

这位朋友	1米90	高	1米85
这件衣服	50公分	长	48公分
这座小山	500米	高	300多米
他家的房子	200平方米	大	150多平方米
这个烤鸭	3斤	重	2斤多

（3）A：有<u>人</u> <u>给你打电话了</u>。

B：是谁？

A：不知道。

人	敲门
一位小姐	在楼下等你
人	找你
几位老人	走过来了

（4）A：<u>中国人</u>叫它什么？

B：<u>中国人</u>叫它"<u>母亲河</u>"。

同学们	他	中国通
南方人	妈妈的母亲	外婆
王小云	那个人	舅舅
他	自己	老画家
队员们	他	王教练

（5）A：<u>他们</u>怎样才<u>会得到好的成绩</u>？

B：<u>他们</u>只要<u>认真准备</u>，就<u>会得到好的成绩</u>。

大家	能学好汉语	认真地练习
他们	可以参加比赛	愿意去
同学们	会有一个健康的身体	每天锻炼

（6）只要<u>你喜欢旅游</u>，<u>每个假期都有地方去</u>。

他提出来	我们都会帮助他
你们欢迎	他们都想参加扭秧歌
你有时间	每天早上都可以来练太极剑

3. 课堂活动　Classroom activities

(1) Ask and answer questions with your classmates about the objects around you to practice the construction "有+多+A".

(2) One student puts forward a condition by using "只要", and other students supply the results by using "就". For example,

　　A：只要不下雨，

　　B：我就在外面跑步。

　　C：公园里就会有很多人。

　　……　……

4. 会话练习　Conversation practice

> **会话常用语 IDIOMATIC EXPRESSIONS IN CONVERSATION**
>
> 不用着急 (Don't worry.)
> 少说也有…… (There are at least...)
> 早在…… (as early as...)
> 像……一样 (to look like...)

【表示鼓励　Giving an encouragement】

　　A：我已经练了少说也有一个多月了，可是还没有学会。真是太难了。

　　B：不用着急，你刚开始学，还不习惯，当然会觉得难。这是很自然的，以后就会容易一些。

　　A：我看我不可能学会了，真不想练了。

　　B：你说到哪儿去了？你已经有了很大的进步，只要你每天都认真地练，就一定能练好。

【询问事物的性状　Asking about the property or state of something】

A：听说泰山是中国最有名的名胜古迹之一，它的面积有多大？

B：它的面积有426平方公里。

A：泰山有多高？

B：它最高的山峰有1545米。唐代的一位诗人（shīrén）说过，"会当凌绝顶，一览众山小"（Huì dāng líng jué dǐng, yì lǎn zhòng shān xiǎo）。意思是说，只要登上泰山最高的山峰，你就会觉得别的山峰又低又小。

5. 看图说话　Describe the following picture

(This is the Guilin landscape of China.)

（名胜　景色　早在　特色　奇怪　变化　像……一样）

6. 交际练习　Communication exercises

（1）Describe the capital of your country to your classmates. Use approximate numbers to describe its area and population, etc.

（2）Describe your favorite scenic spots and historical sites in your country to your classmates.

After you speak, write down what you have said.

阅读与复述 Reading Comprehension and Paraphrasing

🎧20 南水北调 (Nán Shuǐ Běi Diào)

京杭大运河(yùnhé)是世界上最长的运河。它从北京到杭州(Hángzhōu),有1794公里长。京杭大运河跟长城一样,也是中国古代有名的大工程(gōngchéng)。

早在1500多年前,中国人就开始挖(wā)这条运河。那时候的皇帝隋炀帝(Suí Yángdì)三次去江南(Jiāngnán)旅游,都是从运河坐船去的。他还让人们在运河两岸种了很多柳树(liǔshù),因为隋炀帝姓"杨",人们就把这种柳树叫做"杨柳"。

中国的大河,比如长江、黄河,都是从西向东,只有大运河是南北方向,把这些主要的大河连接起来。在中国古代,运河里南来北往的船很多。扬州(Yángzhōu)是长江跟运河汇合(huìhé)的地方,那时候的扬州是一座非常热闹的城市。后来,因为北方雨水少,运河的北段(duàn)早就不能通航(tōngháng)了,只有南段还能通航。

中国北方没有什么大河,水很少;而南方的大河比较多,水也多。经过多年的调查研究(yánjiū),政府打算从扬州把长江的一部分水引(yǐn)到运河,再经过运河向北方送水。这叫"南水北调"。虽然这还只是"南水北调"工程的一部分,但是,它对改善(gǎishàn)北方人民的生活条件是非常重要的。

现在,京杭大运河北京地区的一段已经通航了,人们又看到了古代运河的景色。等到大运河全部通航以后,人们就可以从北京坐船去杭州旅游,看一看运河两岸的景色,了解一下古老而又年轻的运河文化。那该是多么美好的事啊!

三、语法 Grammar

1 "万" 以上的称数法　Numbers over 10,000

In Chinese, the following characters are used to denote the basic numerical units: "个" (one), "十" (ten), "百" (hundred), and "千" (thousand). For the numbers more than ten thousand, the character "万" is used as the basic unit. Thus, we have "万" (ten thousand), "十万" (hundred thousand), "百万" (million), and "千万" (ten million). For the numbers more than one hundred million, the character "亿", eqivalent to "万万", is used as the basic unit. For example,

```
…… 千 百 十 万 千 百 十 万 千 百 十 个
      亿 亿 亿 万 万 万 万
         （亿）
```

　　　　　　1 0 0 0 9　is read as "一万零九" instead of "十千零九"

　　　　　　2 5 0 0 0 0　is read as "二十五万" instead of "二百五十千"

　　　　　　1 7 5 9 9 9 8　is read as "一百七十五万九千九百九十八"

　　　　　　4 1 6 8 3 0 0 0　is read as "四千一百六十八万三千"

　　　　1 3 7 0 0 0 0 0 0 0　is read as "十三亿七千万"

Notes:

❶ All the "zeros" in a multi-digit number are read as a single "零", regardless of how many they actually are. For example, 10,009 is read as "一万零九".

❷ As a rule, when the final digit is "个", "个" can be omitted, while other units cannot. For example, 10,500 is read as "一万零五百".

2 概数　Approximate numbers

（1）用 "几" 表示概数　Using the character "几" to indicate an approximate number

　　几+M+N　　　　　他买了几本书。 (He bought several books.)

　　几+十/百/千/万/亿+M+N　　今年语言学院来了几百个留学生。

(This year, several hundred international students came to the Language Institute.)

十＋几＋M＋N　　前边来了十几个人。

(There are over ten people coming this way.)

这辆车用了二十几万块钱。

(This car cost more than two hundred thousand *kuai*.)

（2）用"多"表示概数　Using the character "多" to indicate an approximate number

A. "多" is placed after an integer more than ten to indicate the remaining sum. For example,

十/百/千/万　＋　多 ＋ M ＋ N/A

10	多	本	词典 (more than ten dictionaries)
1000	多	岁	(more than 1,000 years old)
8800	多	米	高 (more than 8,800 meters high)
1200	多	年	历史 (a history of more than 1,200 years)

B. "多" is placed after the unit or a multi-digit number including the unit's place to indicate the remaining fraction. For example,

Num ＋ M ＋ 多 (＋ N)

两	斤	多	葡萄 (more than two *jin* of grapes)
十四	米	多	白布 (a piece of white cloth more than fourteen meters long)
一	个	多	月 (more than a month)
254	块	多	(more than 254 *kuai*)

（3）Using two adjacent numbers to indicate an approximate number. For example, 一两个，二三十，四五百，六七千，八九万，三四十万.

3 兼语句（2）　Pivotal sentences (2)

The verb "有" can be used to form a pivotal sentence. Here, the object of "有", usually denoting somebody or something that exists, also functions as the subject of the second verb. For this kind of sentence, the subject of the whole sentence is often missing.

Subject	Predicate			
	V₁ "有"	O₁ (S₂)	V₂	O₂
	有	人	敲	门。
	有	多少 人	参加	比赛?
	（没）有	人	给你 打	电话。
	有	几个 朋友	想去	旅游。
黄山	有	一棵 树	叫做	"迎客松"。

4 只要……，就……   The construction "只要……，就……"

"只要" can be placed before or after the subject of the first clause to indicate prerequisite; and "就" (sometimes omitted) introduces the result. For example,

你们只要认真准备，就会得到好的成绩。

同学们只要每天都练，就一定能把字写好。

只要你喜欢旅游，每个假期都有地方去。

只要天气好，我们就一定去。

四、字与词 Chinese Characters and Words

构词法（5）：主谓式

Word formation method (5): Subject-predicate compound words

The latter character states the meaning of the former one, e.g. "年 + 轻→年轻". Other examples, 圣诞, 水平 and 头疼.

Rivers and Lakes in China

China has numerous rivers and lakes and is rich in natural resources.

Most of the rivers in China rise in the Qinghai-Tibet Plateau in western China and flow eastwards into the sea. The big drop in elevation generates plenty of waterpower resources, the reserves of which amount to 680 million kilowatts, ranking first in the world. The drainage area of the rivers flowing outward such as Yangtze River, Yellow River, Heilongjiang River, Zhujiang River, Liao River, Yalu Tsangpo River and Irtysh River accounts for 64% of China's total land area, while that of the inland rivers that flow into lakes or end in deserts accounts for 36%. The longest inland river of China is the Tarim River in the Xinjiang Uygur Autonomous Region.

As we have already learned in Book 1, Yangtze River and Yellow River are the two biggest rivers in China. Yangtze River is the longest river in China and the third longest in the world; and Yellow River, the second longest in China, is one of the cradles of ancient Chinese civilizations. Besides them, the most famous big rivers in southern and northern China are Zhujiang River and Heilongjiang River respectively.

Apart from the natural rivers, there is also the Grand Canal, a well-known man-made river in China. First dug in the 5th century B.C., it starts from Beijing and goes

southwards to Hangzhou, linking up five major river systems in China. It is the earliest and longest man-made river in the world.

There are more than 20,000 lakes in China, which, however, distribute unevenly among regions. In general, the biggest freshwater lakes are found in eastern China, especially in the middle and lower reaches of Yangtze River; in western China, Qinghai-Tibet Plateau is the area abounding with lakes, which are mostly inland salt-water ones. China has been famous for its "five lakes and four seas" since ancient times, among which the "five lakes" refer to Dongting Lake in Hunan Province, Poyang Lake in Jiangxi Province, Taihu Lake and Hongze Lake in Jiangsu Province and Chaohu Lake in Anhui Province.

第三十二课
Lesson
32

复习 Review

这样的问题现在也不能问了

Nowadays such questions are not supposed
to be asked any more.

While climbing Mt. Huang, Ma Dawei came
across a Chinese traveler who asked him some
personal questions considered inappropriate in the
West. Curious about the different cultural views
on privacy, Ma Dawei asked him some similar
questions on purpose.

第三十二课 （复习）这样的问题现在也不能问了 101

Lesson 32　(Review) Nowadays such questions are not supposed to be asked any more.

一、课文　Text

🎧 21 （一）

马大为：请问，从这条小路能上山顶吗？

小伙子：我想可以。我也要上去，咱们一起往上爬吧。

马大为：好啊！

小伙子：您第一次游览黄山吧？您怎么称呼？①

认识
Getting acquainted with somebody

马大为：我叫马大为。

小伙子：太巧了，我也姓马，你叫我小马吧。②

猜测
Guessing

　　　　我看你的岁数跟我差不多，③ 可能大一点儿。你今年有二十五六了吧？

马大为：你就叫我老马吧。

小伙子：你在哪儿工作？

马大为：我还在读书呢。④

小伙子：哦，你是留学生。你汉语说得真棒！

马大为：很一般。

小伙子：我见过几位老外，他们汉语说得没有你好，你说得最好。你
　　　　们来中国留学，父母还得给你们很多钱吧？

马大为：不一定。

小伙子：那你得一边学习一边挣钱了？结婚了没有？

马大为：你累不累？我又热又累，咱们喝点儿水吧。我说小马，你在
　　　　哪儿工作？

小伙子：我在一家网络公司工作。

马大为：哦，你是搞网络的，工资一定很高吧？

小伙子：不算太高。⑤

模糊表达
Giving a vague response

马大为：我想只要在高新技术企业工作，收入就不会低。

小伙子：那也得看公司和个人的情况。⑥

马大为：你们公司怎么样？

小伙子：还行吧。⑦

马大为：你的收入一定不低了？

小伙子：我去年才开始工作，收入还凑合。

马大为："还凑合"是什么意思？

小伙子：就是"马马虎虎"的意思。

马大为：啊！你看，那边围着很多人，那不是迎客松吗？

小伙子：是，就是那棵迎客松。大家都在那儿照相呢，咱们也去照张

相吧。

马大为：好啊！

生词 New Words

1. 游览	yóulǎn	V	to go sight-seeing, to tour　游览黄山，游览长城，游览海南岛
览	lǎn		to look at, to see
2. 称呼	chēnghu	V/N	to call; a form of address　怎么称呼；正式的称呼，一般的称呼
称	chēng	V	to call　称他老师，称自己小马
3. 巧	qiǎo	A	by chance, coincidental, skillful　太巧了，真巧，巧极了，她很巧
4. 差不多	chàbuduō	A/Adv	about the same; almost　岁数跟我差不多；差不多都问到了
5. 读书	dúshū	VO	to study, to read a book　还在读书，在中学读书，读了很多书，读完这本书
读	dú	V	to read, to study　读《红楼梦》，读外语，读大学
6. 哦	ò	Int	oh, aha (expressing a sudden realization)　哦，是你；哦，是这样

7.	棒	bàng	A	(coll.) awesome 真棒，太棒了，棒极了
8.	留学	liúxué	VO	to study abroad 来中国留学，出国留学，留了几年学
9.	父母	fùmǔ	N	father and mother, parents 我的父母
	父	fù		father
10.	挣	zhèng	V	to earn 挣钱，挣多少钱
11.	结婚	jiéhūn	VO	to marry 结婚了没有，跟谁结婚
12.	网络	wǎngluò	N	Internet 网络公司
13.	搞	gǎo	V	to engage in 搞网络，搞美术，搞音乐
14.	工资	gōngzī	N	salary 挣工资，拿工资，给工资
15.	算	suàn	V	to consider, to regard as 不算高，不算多
16.	高新技术	gāoxīn jìshù		high technology 搞高新技术
17.	企业	qǐyè	N	enterprise 高新技术企业，中小企业，企业管理
18.	个人	gèrén	N	individual (person) 个人的情况，个人的事情，我个人
19.	凑合	còuhe	V	(coll.) to make do, to be passable, to be not too bad 还凑合，收入还凑合，电影还凑合
20.	照相	zhàoxiàng	VO	to take a picture 照（一）张相

注释 Notes

① 您怎么称呼？

"May I have your name, please?"

This expression is used to politely ask someone's name. In response, one may say "我姓……，叫……".

第三十二课 （复习）这样的问题现在也不能问了 105

Lesson 32 (Review) Nowadays such questions are not supposed to be asked any more.

② 你叫我小马吧。

"Please call me Xiao Ma."

Either "小" or "老" can be placed before a monosyllabic surname. For example, "老张" or "小王" is not so formal as "张先生" or "王小姐". This is a general way of addressing friends or acquaintances. "小+surname" is normally used when addressing young people, whereas "老+surname" is used when addressing the middle-aged or the elderly. When Ma Dawei says "你就叫我 '老马' 吧", he is joking. Note: When addressing one's family members, relatives or people with higher social status, "小" or "老" is not used.

③ 我看你的岁数跟我差不多。

"It looks like that you and I are about the same age."

As an adjective, "差不多" often functions as a predicate, meaning "about the same, similar". For example,

这个故事跟那个故事差不多。

这两件衣服样子差不多。

As an adverb, "差不多" is usually used before a verb or an adjective, meaning "almost, nearly". For example,

黄山的名胜古迹我差不多都去了。

大家差不多走了两个小时。

他和我差不多高。

④ 我还在读书呢。

"I am still studying in school."

Here, "读书" means "to study in school, to pursue education". For example,

王小云没有工作，她还在语言学院读书呢。

她弟弟现在还在中学读书呢。

⑤ 不算太高。

"Not too much."

"算" usually means "to consider or regard as". Sometimes the verb "是" can be added to "算". For example,

今天不算热。

他这次考试算是很好了。

⑥ 那也得看公司和个人的情况。

"That also depends on the performance of the company and yourself." Here, "看" means "to depend on". For example,

明天去不去游览，得看天气情况。

考试成绩好不好，得看准备得怎么样。

⑦ 还行吧。

"Not bad."

The adverb "还" (5) means "passably", implying that something is neither good nor bad. For example, 还可以，还好，还不错，还凑合.

🎧 22 (二)

宋　华：这次旅游怎么样？

马大为：好极了，黄山的名胜古迹我差不多都欣赏了。美丽的黄山真是名不虚传。

宋　华："名不虚传"用得真地道。

马大为：这是跟一起旅行的中国朋友学的。不过，聊天儿的时候，几个中国朋友把我围在中间，问了很多问题，问得我没办法回答。

宋　华：他们问了你一些什么问题？

马大为：差不多把个人的隐私都问到了。比如，问我多大、家里有几口人、每月挣多少钱、结婚没有、有没有住房什么的。⑧ 对了，还问我的背包是多少钱买的。

宋　华：这是关心你嘛！

马大为：可是我们认为这些都是个人的隐私。别人愿意说，你可以听着；如果别人不想说，这些问题就不能问。

第三十二课 （复习）这样的问题现在也不能问了 107

Lesson 32 (Review) Nowadays such questions are not supposed to be asked any more.

宋　华：对这些问题，我们的看法是不太一样。我们认为，问这些只

表示友好和关心。

马大为：我拿多少工资是我自己的事儿，他为什么要知道？我被他们

问得不知道该怎么办，这哪儿是关心？

宋　华：问问题的小伙子可能很少见到外国人，他

有点儿好奇，就问得多一些。你知道吗？

中国人以前收入都不太高，收入当然是最重要的一件事儿。

所以互相问工资是表示关心。

解释
Explaining

马大为：哦，是这样。可是，我问那个小伙子每月挣多少钱，他也不

愿意把他的工资收入清清楚楚地告诉我。

宋　华：可以说以前这不是隐私，可是现在是了，这样的问题现在也

不能问了。不过，这也是向西方文化学的。

马大为：你们学得真快。宋华，今天我也想关心你一下：你爸爸、妈

妈每月有多少工资，你能告诉我吗？

宋　华：可以。"比上不足，比下有余"，够花了。⑨

生词 New Words

1. 欣赏	xīnshǎng	V	to appreciate, to enjoy	欣赏自然景色，欣赏音乐，欣赏越剧，欣赏书法，欣赏字画
2. 美丽	měilì	A	beautiful	美丽的黄山，美丽的姑娘，美丽的月亮，美丽的大海

3.	名不虚传	míng bù xū chuán	IE	to deserve the reputation	真是名不虚传
4.	地道	dìdao	A	pure, typical, genuine	用得真地道，说得很地道，地道的汉语，地道的上海话
5.	中间	zhōngjiān	N	middle, center	围在中间，坐在中间，客厅中间，舞台中间，书房中间
6.	办法	bànfǎ	N	way, method	有办法，没办法，用什么办法，想一个办法
7.	隐私	yǐnsī	N	privacy	个人的隐私，了解别人的隐私
8.	住房	zhùfáng	N	house, housing	有没有住房，住房有多大，住房问题
9.	什么的	shénmede	Pt	(coll.) and so on	书、报、本子什么的，结婚没有、有没有住房什么的
10.	背包	bēibāo	N	knapsack, backpack	名牌背包，一个背包
	背	bēi	V	to carry	背东西
	包	bāo	N	bag, satchel	书包
11.	关心	guānxīn	V	to be concerned with	关心你，关心别人，关心这件事儿，关心世界，表示关心
12.	认为	rènwéi	V	to think, to consider	我认为很好
13.	友好	yǒuhǎo	A	friendly	表示友好，友好的国家，对他们很友好
14.	好奇	hàoqí	A	curious	有点儿好奇，对外国风俗好奇
15.	清楚	qīngchu	A	clear	说得很清楚，写得很清楚，清清楚楚地告诉我
16.	比上不足，比下有余	bǐ shàng bùzú, bǐ xià yǒuyú	IE	better than some, though not as good as others	
17.	够	gòu	V/Adv	to be adequate; enough, sufficiently	够用，够吃，够住，够高；够忙的，不够热闹
*18.	花	huā	V	to spend	不够花，花钱，花时间

第三十二课 （复习）这样的问题现在也不能问了 109

Lesson 32 (Review) Nowadays such questions are not supposed to be asked any more.

补充生词 Supplementary Words

1. 工程师	gōngchéngshī	N	engineer
2. 滑	huá	V	to slide
3. 王兴	Wáng Xīng	PN	Wang Xing (a person's name)
4. 外资	wàizī	N	foreign capital
5. 部门	bùmén	N	department
6. 贷款	dàikuǎn	VO/N	to provide or ask for a loan; loan
7. 竞争	jìngzhēng	V	to compete
8. 激烈	jīliè	A	intense
9. 工具	gōngjù	N	tool
10. 经验	jīngyàn	N	experience
11. 学历	xuélì	N	record of formal schooling, educational back-ground
12. 淘汰	táotài	V	to eliminate through selection or competition
13. 支持	zhīchí	V	to support
14. 前途	qiántú	N	future

注释　Notes

⑧ 问我多大、家里有几口人、每月挣多少钱、结婚没有、有没有住房什么的。

"Ask about my age, family members, salary, marital status, housing condition, and so forth."

"什么的" is used after a phrase or a series of parallel phrases to mean "and so on". It is often used in spoken Chinese. For example,

我喜欢听中国民族音乐什么的。

星期六他常去看电影、听音乐、唱京剧什么的。

Note: The words and expressions in this lesson: 棒, 还行 and 还凑合 are also frequently used in spoken Chinese.

⑨ 够花了。

"Fairly enough."

"够 + V" indicates having reached the amount needed. The verb is usually a monosyllabic one. For example,

他每月的工资够用了。

我们带两瓶水够喝了。

"够 + A" indicates having reached a standard or degree. For example,

这块布够长了，可以做一件衣服。

他已经够忙了，你别再去麻烦他了。

二、练习　Exercises

练习与运用　Drills and Practice 23

核心句 KEY SENTENCES

1. 您怎么称呼?
2. 你的岁数跟我差不多。
3. 你汉语说得真棒!
4. 工资不算太高。
5. 那也得看公司和个人的情况。
6. 差不多把个人的隐私都问到了。
7. 问我多大、结婚没有、有没有住房什么的。
8. 我被他们问得不知道该怎么办。

1. 熟读下列词组 Read the following phrases until you learn them by heart

（1）跟演员差不多　　跟司机差不多　　跟老师写的差不多

跟我花的差不多　　差不多都复习了　　差不多都来了

差不多游览了一个星期　　　差不多花了2000块钱

（2） 搞艺术的　　搞武术的　　搞高新技术的　　搞管理工作的

　　　搞展览　　　搞活动　　　搞一个比赛　　　搞一个聚会

（3） 不算好　　不算晚　　不算太低　　不算漂亮　　不算干净

　　　算不错　　算可以　　算很努力　　算比较地道　　算最便宜

（4） 得看天气好不好　　　得看时间够不够　　　得看人多不多

　　　得看工作忙不忙　　　得看身体好不好　　　得看大家的意见怎么样

2. 句型替换 Pattern drills

（1） A：网络公司的收入怎么样？

　　 B：网络公司的收入跟这个企业差不多。

这件衣服的样子　　那个商店卖的
这个故事　　　　　我读过的
她每月花的钱　　　我花的
他唱京剧　　　　　演员唱的

（2） A：他游览黄山的名胜古迹了没有？

　　 B：他差不多都游览了。

修整那些盆景　　都修整完了
欣赏这些字画　　欣赏了一个上午
请他的好朋友来　　都请来了
结婚　　　　　　结婚两年了

（3） A：他们问你问题了吗？

　　 B：问了，我被他们问得真没办法
　　　　回答。

聊天儿　　聊　　看书
跳舞　　　跳　　睡觉
敲锣打鼓　敲　　休息

（4）A：他做什么工作？

　　　B：他是搞网络的，是个一般工作人员。

艺术	书法家
高新技术	工程师（gōngchéngshī）
管理工作	经理
武术	教练

（5）A：我带了1000块钱，够不够？

　　　B：我看够花了。

准备	20瓶水	喝
买	50张纸	画
借	6本小说	看
租	10张光盘	听

3. 课堂活动　Classroom activities

（1）One student asks a question, and another student replies by listing a number of things, ending with "什么的". For example,

　　A：你喜欢吃什么中餐？

　　B：我喜欢吃烤鸭、涮羊肉、点心什么的。

（2）One student names something of everyday use (such as a book, a movie and some product), and other students comment on it using the following words or phrases that indicate degrees:

好极了，最好，太好了，太棒了

非常好，实在好，真好，真棒，很好

比较好，不错，还好，还可以，还行，还凑合，马马虎虎，不太好

不好，差，糟糕，坏

4. 会话练习 Conversation practice

会话常用语 IDIOMATIC EXPRESSIONS IN CONVERSATION

您怎么称呼 (May I have your name, please?)

真棒 (Great.)

不算太高 (Not so high / tall.)

得看…… (It depends on...)

还行 (Not bad.)

还凑合 (Not too bad.)

……什么的 (...and so on, and so forth)

【认识　Getting acquainted with somebody】

A：请问，您怎么称呼？

B：我姓丁，叫丁强。

A：丁先生做什么工作？

B：别客气，就叫我小丁吧。我是搞旅游的。

【猜测　Guessing】

A：您是搞武术的吧？

B：对，我是武术教练。

A：您一定能教太极剑吧？

B：当然。谁要学？

A：我们这儿有一些武术爱好者，他们对太极剑很感兴趣。如果每星期学两次，每次一小时，一个月的时间差不多够了吧？

B：一共8个小时不够，少说也要16个小时。

【模糊表达　Giving a vague response】

A：老张，你们公司去年的收入很好吧？

B：还行。

A: 工作人员的工资一定提高得很快。

B: 不一定。得看个人的工作情况。

A: 听说你们单位今年要进不少人。

B: 不算太多，跟去年差不多。

A: 我看今年你们公司会有很大的发展。

B: 一般吧。

【解释　Explaining】

A: 小王，什么事情让你不高兴?

B: 上午经理找我了，他问了我很多问题，好像我做错了事儿。

A: 他是关心你，可能他也想了解一下公司的情况。

B: 可是这些事儿跟我没有关系。

A: 经理刚从国外回来。你知道吗? 最近大家对公司有不少意见。经理要跟每个人都聊一聊，可能是想了解大家的看法。他也找我聊了。

5. 看图说话　Describe the following pictures

❶ 跟……一样　跟……差不多　跟……不一样　　❷ 有/没有　热情

❸ 很/更/最 高

❹ 比　优美

❺ 有　是

❻ 站/坐/躺/等　着

❼ 爬　滑(huá)　坐　走　跑　　上来　下去　过来　进来　进去

6. 交际练习 Communication exercises

(1) Someone who has promised to come to a party has not arrived yet, and those who are present start to make guesses what might have happened to him/her.

(2) After the party, explain on behalf of the person who did not show up, why he/she failed to come.

After you speak, write down what you have said.

阅读与复述 Reading Comprehension and Paraphrasing

24 经理上学

　　王兴（Wáng Xīng）今年35岁，在一家外资（wàizī）企业工作，是一个部门（bùmén）的经理。他妻子跟他在同一个企业工作，他们有一个可爱的孩子。去年，王兴向银行贷款（dàikuǎn）买了一套房子，今年又买了小汽车，生活过得很不错。王兴想的最多的就是怎么挣更多的钱。

　　可是，最近王兴忙得休息的时间也没有了。他不再像过去那样，每到星期六就跟朋友们一起吃饭、聊天儿、唱歌、跳舞。他又去上学了，上了一个工商管理班。他自己交了10万块钱的学费，还加上每个星期六、星期天的休息时间。

　　王兴已经是经理了，为什么还要去读书呢？这是因为他感到竞争（jìngzhēng）越来越激烈（jīliè）了。他常跟妻子说："我在大学只学了英语，没有学过工商管理专业。可是外语只是一种工具（gōngjù），现在会英语的人也越来越多了。大学毕业以后，我换了五六家公司，虽然有了不少工作经验（jīngyàn），但说到管理的专业知识，有很多都是我不知道的。特别是中国加入WTO以后，更感到自己知道得太少了。

现在来我们公司找工作的年轻人，学历（xuélì）越来越高，知识也越来越新。跟他们相比，我现在有的那些知识和经验已经不够用了。如果再不学习，很快就有被淘汰（táotài）的可能。所以我要再去学点儿新东西。"王兴的想法得到了妻子的支持（zhīchí），她希望他在今后的竞争中能有更好的前途（qiántú）。

三、语法复习　Grammar Review

1　结构助词"的、地、得"　The structural particles "的、地、得"

(1) Used between the attributive modifier and the modified word, "的" is the indicator of an attributive.

① "的" is used as the attributive modifier to indicate the ownership of the modified word. For example,

> 爸爸的西服
>
> 图书馆的书

If an attributive noun is used to indicate the property of the modified word, "的" is usually omitted. For example,

> 中国人
>
> 语言学院
>
> 英语词典

② When a personal pronoun is used as the attributive modifier to indicate the ownership, "的" is generally used. For example,

> 他的车
>
> 大家的看法

If the modified word denotes a family member, a relative, or a place where one works, "的" is often omitted. For example,

> 她妈妈
>
> 我们学院

③ When a disyllabic adjective, an adjectival phrase, or the reduplicative form of an adjective is used as the attributive modifier, "的" is generally used. For example,

年轻的姑娘

最好的小伙子

很漂亮的围巾

干干净净的宿舍

When the attributive modifier is a monosyllabic adjective, "的" is usually omitted. For example,

男朋友

新汽车

大背包

④ When the attributive modifier is a verb or a verbal phrase, "的" is usually used. For example,

工作的时候

来参观的学生

给妹妹买的礼物

在家里打的电话

⑤ When a subject-predicate phrase acts as the attributive modifier, "的" is generally used. For example,

宋华买的蛋糕

她送的花儿

头疼的病人

⑥ "的" is often used when the attributive modifier is a prepositional phrase. For example,

对学校的意见

往北的公共汽车

The word order in a multiple-modifier attributive,

Pr	+	这/那	+	Num-MP	+	A	+	N	+	Modified word
										词典
								汉语		词典
							新	汉语		词典
				两 本		新		汉语		词典
		那		两 本		新		汉语		词典
我的		那		两 本		新		汉语		词典
indicating the ownership		demonstrative pronoun		indicating the quantity		indicating the attribute		indicating the property		modified word

(2) Used between an adverbial modifier and the predicate verb, "地" is the indicator of an adverbial.

"地" is usually used in a descriptive adverbial, which is a disyllabic adjective, an adjectival phrase or the reduplicative form of an adjective. For example,

> 热情地欢迎
>
> 非常努力地学习
>
> 认认真真地工作

However, when a monosyllabic adjective is used as the adverbial, "地" is generally omitted. For example,

> 慢走
>
> 多演奏
>
> 早回家

(3) Used between the predicate verb or an adjective and a complement of degree or a modal complement, "得" is the indicator of a complement. For example,

① V/A + "得" + modal complement

> 跑得很快
>
> 写得更漂亮
>
> 高兴得跳了起来

② V/A + "得" + complement of degree

喜欢得很

忙得很

舒服得多

2 "把" 字句小结   Summary of the "把" sentence

（1）S + 把 + O把 + V + 在/到/给/成 + O

他们把大块的食物放在盘子里。

宋华把客人送到车站。

丁力波把他买的京剧票送给王小云了。

他把这本书翻译成英文了。

（2）S + 把 + O把 + V + Complement

林娜把今天的练习做完了。(resultative complement)

王小云把照相机带回家去了。(directional complement)

她把杯子洗得干干净净的。(modal complement)

他把你写的信看了两遍。(complement of frequency)

（3）S + 把 + O把 + V + Other elements

你把这杯酒喝了。(verb plus the perfective aspect word "了")

您把语言学院的情况给我们介绍介绍。(reduplicated verb)

Notes:

(1) The construction "V + 在/到/成/给 + O" requires the use of the "把" sentence.

(2) In order to emphasize the result of the action that is performed by the verb upon the object, the "把" sentence is usually used, as shown in (2) and (3) above.

(3) Negative adverbs or optative verbs must be placed before "把". For example,

她没有把你给她买的礼物送给妹妹。

王小云想把这本书翻译成中文。

第三十二课 （复习）这样的问题现在也不能问了 121

Lesson 32 (Review) Nowadays such questions are not supposed to be asked any more.

3 副词 "就" 和 "还"   The adverbs "就" and "还"

"就" is used:

(1) to stress a fact; e.g.

这就是张教授。

我就买这件。

(2) to stress that something happens early or quickly; e.g.

刚七点，他就来了。

我马上就回来。

(3) to show that two actions happen in a sequence; e.g.

他们觉得有点儿累，就坐下来休息一会儿。

今天的课文我不太懂，就去问老师。

(4) to show that one thing happens immediately after another; e.g.

我下了课就去买盆花儿。

他们吃了晚饭就去公园散步。

(5) to indicate that something is going to happen soon; e.g.

就要下雨了。

就要放假了。

"还" is used:

(1) to include additional remarks; e.g.

他喜欢书法，还喜欢京剧。

大家还有问题吗?

(2) to show that an action is still going on; e.g.

已经十一点了，他还在做练习。

你明年还想学中文吗?

(3) to mean "barely, scarcely"; e.g.

他的成绩还可以。

这个电影还行。

(4) to indicate a higher degree; e.g.

他比他哥哥还高。

我丢了自行车，他比我还着急。

(5) to show that something is unexpected; e.g.

张教授还是个书法家呢！

他还画过油画呢！

四、字与词　Chinese Characters and Words

构词法（6）：重叠式
Word formation method (6): Reduplicated compound words

① The meaning of the word is exactly the same as that of the character. For example, 妈妈, 爸爸, 哥哥, 弟弟, 姐姐, 妹妹, 舅舅.

② The meaning of the word is basically the same as that of the character. For example, 刚刚, 常常, 轻轻.

Chinese People's Verbal Communication

Language is a tool for communication; it reflects the culture of a country or region. Chinese language is no exception.

Chinese people used to call each other "同志" (comrade), a form of address which is barely heard today. Over the recent decades, "女士" (madam) and "先生" (sir) have been used more often. To address an elder person who is not a relative, Chinese people may use "伯伯" (father's elder brother), "叔叔" (father's younger brother) or "阿姨" (mother's sister), etc. Different from that in English, in Chinese, one can also be addressed using "老师" (Teacher), "经理" (Manager), or "医生" (Doctor), etc., together with the surname, such as "张老师" or "王经理".

When exchanging greetings, Chinese people think it is sincere to ask some personal questions concerning one's age, marriage and family. They also tend to express their concern for someone by asking such questions as "你去哪儿 (Where are you going)?" and "你在做什么 (What are you doing)?" When a guest is leaving, a Chinese host would escort him/her outside the gate or even to the street. The guest would say "请留步", meaning "Don't bother to go any further", and the host is supposed to say "走好" (Watch your step), "慢走" (Take your time) or "再来啊" (Please come back again), etc.

When being praised, a Chinese person often shows modesty by saying "哪里哪里" or "您过奖了", meaning "You are flattering me, and I don't really deserve the compliment". Generally speaking, Chinese people seldom say "谢谢" (Thank you) to their relatives or friends, otherwise both parties would feel uncomfortable with the emotional distance.

If you want to learn Chinese well, it's necessary for you to learn about the culture of verbal communication embodied in Chinese language.

第三十三课
Lesson
33

保护环境就是保护我们自己

Protecting the environment means protecting ourselves.

Lin Na, Wang Xiaoyun and their friends go to the suburbs of Beijing to visit Mt. Ling. They enjoy the scenery, which is similar to that of the Tibetan Plateau. Then they visit the Tibetan Botanical Garden, which was developed by a female scientist, and they discuss many environmental issues.

一、课文　Text

🎧 25 （一）

陆雨平：好，灵山到了。

王小云：车还上得去吗？

陆雨平：上不去了，请下车吧！你们先往山上走。我把车停好，马上
　　　　就来。

林　娜：这儿空气真好。

陆雨平：林娜、小云，山很高，你们爬得上
　　　　去吗？

> 表示可能
> **Indicating a possibility**

王小云：没问题，我们一步一步地往上爬吧。

宋　华：你们可能不知道，灵山是北京最高的地方。有位女科学家发现，这儿的自然环境跟西藏高原差不多。

林　娜：好啊，今天我们来参观灵山的藏趣园，就可以欣赏一下西藏的高原景色了。

马大为：藏趣园是不是国家公园？

王小云：不是。藏趣园是那位女科学家建立的一个植物园，年年都有很多中小学生来这儿过夏令营。[①] 学生们在这样的环境里，既能欣赏自然景色，又能接受保护环境的教育。

丁力波：这个好主意是怎么想出来的？

王小云：那位女科学家在西藏工作了18年。1996年，她退休了，想在北京找一个地方继续她的科学研究。因为灵山的自然条件很像西藏高原，她就把西藏的一些植物移植到这儿来。她还盖了一个在西藏住过的那种小木屋。你看见了吗？小木屋就在前边！

林　娜：在哪儿呢？我怎么看不见？哦，是不是那棵大树旁边的屋子？

王小云：对。网上有一篇文章叫《小木屋》，你读过吗？那就是写这位女科学家的。

林　娜：没读过。我现在还看不懂中文网上的长文章。

生词 New Words

1. 保护	bǎohù	V	to protect	保护小孩儿，保护老人，保护字画
2. 环境	huánjìng	N	environment	保护环境，生活环境，学习环境，城市环境
3. 空气	kōngqì	N	air	空气好，空气不好
4. 步	bù	M	step	一步一步地，两步，走一步
5. 科学家	kēxuéjiā	N	scientist	女科学家，重要的科学家
科学	kēxué	N	science	学习科学，科学工作，科学活动
6. 高原	gāoyuán	N	plateau, highland	高原景色，西藏高原
7. 建立	jiànlì	V	to set up, to establish	建立学校，建立医院，建立博物馆，建立剧团，建立国家公园
8. 植物园	zhíwùyuán	N	botanical garden	建立植物园，参观植物园，游览植物园
植物	zhíwù	N	plant	喜欢植物，保护植物
9. 夏令营	xiàlìngyíng	N	summer camp	过夏令营，参加夏令营，举办夏令营
10. 既……又……	jì……yòu……		both ... and ...	
11. 接受	jiēshòu	V	to accept	接受礼物，接受意见，接受帮助，接受检查
受	shòu	V	to receive, to be subjected to	
12. 教育	jiàoyù	V/N	to educate; education	教育学生；接受教育，大学教育，保护环境的教育
13. 主意	zhǔyi	N	idea	好主意，他的主意，奇怪的主意，有一个主意
14. 继续	jìxù	V	to continue	继续学习，继续看电视，继续下棋，继续聊天儿

15.	研究	yánjiū	V	to study, to research　研究汉语，研究文学，研究这件事儿，研究问题，继续研究，科学研究，对汉语很有研究
16.	条件	tiáojiàn	N	condition　自然条件，工作条件，学习条件，生活条件
17.	移植	yízhí	V	to transplant　移植花儿，移植盆景，移植君子兰，移植植物
	移	yí	V	to move
18.	木屋	mùwū	N	log cabin　小木屋
	木（头）	mù (tou)		wood
	屋（子）	wū (zi)	N	house, room
19.	看见	kànjiàn	VC	to see, to catch sight of　看见月亮，看见山，看见他，看见迎客松
20.	网	wǎng	N	net　网上，上网
21.	灵山	Líng Shān	PN	Mt. Ling (a mountain in the suburbs of Beijing)
22.	藏趣园	Zàngqùyuán	PN	the Tibetan Botanical Garden

注释　Note

① 年年都有很多中小学生来这儿过夏令营。

"Many primary and middle school students come here every year to attend the summer camp."

"中小学生" is the abbreviation of "中学生和小学生". Similarly, "中国学生和外国学生" can be abbreviated as "中外学生"; "北京大学" as "北大"; and "环境保护" as "环保". Note that one cannot just abbreviate at will. For example, "北京郊区" can be abbreviated as "京郊", but not as "北郊", because "北郊" means "北部郊区" (northern outskirts).

🎧 26 （二）

陆雨平：今天的报纸来了，我写的植树节的消息登出来了。②

王小云：我看看。那天很多人都去郊区植树，一些外国人也参加了。

陆雨平：现在人人都关心北京的绿化，③ 因为保护环境是非常重要的
　　　　事儿。

林　娜：我最担心空气污染。还有，听说沙漠正一年一年地向北京靠
　　　　近，最近的地方离北京还不到100公
　　　　里。④ 这真是个大问题啊。

表示担心
Expressing concern

马大为：北京市正在努力解决空气污染的问题。我们也感觉得出来，
　　　　现在这儿的空气比我们刚来的时候好多了。

陆雨平：看得出来，你们也很关心北京的环保问题。现在，种树是保
　　　　护环境的重要办法之一。北京有不少种纪念树的活动，比如
　　　　说，种结婚纪念树、生日纪念树、全家纪念树什么的。大家

不但要把树种上，而且棵棵都要种活。我的这篇文章就是写一位非洲外交官参加种树的事儿。这位外交官很喜欢北京，植树节那天，他带着全家人种了一棵"友谊树"。在北京的外交官们都喜欢一家一家地去参加这种活动。

林　娜：你们来看，这几张照片是大为拍的。这张照片上是一位老人和他的小孙子在种树。一棵一棵的小树排得多整齐啊！天上的白云也照上了，照得真美！

王小云：张张照片都拍得很好。想不到，大为照相的技术还真不错。

林　娜：你知道吗？大为的作品还参加过展览呢。

引起话题
Bringing up a topic

陆雨平：这些照片确实很好，应该在报上登出来，让更多的人知道种树多么重要。

林　娜：北京既是中国的首都，又是世界有名的大都市。保护北京的环境，跟每个在北京生活的人都有关系。⑤

马大为：你说得很对。保护环境就是保护我们自己。

生词 New Words

1. 登	dēng	V	to publish (an essay, article, etc.)	登文章，登小说，登出来，登在报上
2. 绿化	lǜhuà	V	to make (a place) green by planting trees, to afforest	绿化北京，绿化环境
3. 沙漠	shāmò	N	desert	沙漠化

4.	靠近	kàojìn	V	to draw near, to approach 靠近学校，靠近墙，靠近大门，靠近北京，向北京靠近
	近	jìn	A	near, close 最近的地方
5.	市	shì	N	city, municipality 北京市，上海市
6.	解决	jiějué	V	to solve 解决问题，解决的办法
7.	污染	wūrǎn	V	to pollute 空气污染，环境污染，解决污染的问题
*8.	纪念	jìniàn	V	to commemorate 纪念品，纪念树，纪念这位文学家，纪念活动
9.	活	huó	V	to live 活的花儿，活的树，活的虾，种活，养活
10.	外交官	wàijiāoguān	N	diplomat 非洲外交官，在北京的外交官们
	外交	wàijiāo	N	diplomacy 外交人员，外交工作，外交活动
11.	确实	quèshí	Adv	really, indeed 确实很好，确实不错
12.	首都	shǒudū	N	capital 中国的首都，国家的首都
13.	都市	dūshì	N	big city, metropolis 大都市，有名的都市
14.	关系	guānxì	N	relation, relationship 跟每个人都有关系，没关系，建立外交关系，关系很好
15.	植树节	Zhíshù Jié	PN	Arbor Day
	植树	zhíshù	VO	to plant trees 到山上植树
16.	非洲	Fēizhōu	PN	Africa

补充生词 Supplementary Words

1.	熊猫	xióngmāo	N	panda
	熊	xióng	N	bear
	猫	māo	N	cat
2.	珍稀	zhēnxī	A	rare
3.	抢救	qiǎngjiù	V	to save, to rescue
4.	中国野生	Zhōngguó Yěshēng	PN	China Wildlife Conservation
	动物保护协会	Dòngwù Bǎohù Xiéhuì		Association

5.	决定	juédìng	V	to decide
6.	动物园	dòngwùyuán	N	zoo
7.	竹叶	zhú yè		bamboo leaf
8.	胖	pàng	A	fat
9.	腿	tuǐ	N	leg
10.	耳朵	ěrduo	N	ear
11.	墨镜	mòjìng	N	sunglasses
12.	留	liú	V	to stay
13.	使者	shǐzhě	N	envoy

注释　Notes

② 我写的植树节的消息登出来了。

"My article on Arbor Day was published in the newspaper."

In China, Arbor Day is on March 12th.

③ 现在人人都关心北京的绿化。

"Now everyone is concerned with the afforestation of Beijing."

Some adjectives or nouns can combine with the suffix "化" to indicate to change into the attribute or state presented by the adjectives or nouns. For example, 绿化，美化，净化，简化，正常化，一般化，中国化，欧化，儿化. Sometimes, "A/N+化+N" can form a noun, such as "简化字" (simplified characters).

④ 听说沙漠正一年一年地向北京靠近，最近的地方离北京还不到100公里。

"It is said that the desert is drawing near to Beijing year by year. The closest point is no less than 100 km away from Beijing."

The verb "到" means "达到" (to arrive, to reach). "到" is followed by a numeral-measure word phrase. "（不）到+Num-MP" means that a certain quantity has (or has not) been reached. For example,

这一课的生词还不到40个。

他到三十岁了吧?

"正+V+呢" also means that an action is going on. For example,

我去他家的时候，他正看电视呢。

⑤ 保护北京的环境，跟每个在北京生活的人都有关系。

"Protecting the environment of Beijing is related to everyone who lives in Beijing."

"跟+N/Pr+有/没（有）关系" is often used to indicate being or not being related to something. For example,

环保问题跟每个人都有关系。

他跟这事儿没有关系。

这件事儿跟你有没有关系？

这事儿跟我有什么关系？

二、练习　Exercises

练习与运用　Drills and Practice 27

核心句 KEY SENTENCES

1. 你们爬得上去吗？
2. 这个好主意是怎么想出来的？
3. 我现在还看不懂中文网上的长文章。
4. 现在人人都关心北京的绿化。
5. 听说沙漠正一年一年地向北京靠近。
6. 最近的地方离北京还不到100公里。
7. 我们也感觉得出来。
8. 北京既是中国的首都，又是世界有名的大都市。
9. 保护北京的环境，跟每个在北京生活的人都有关系。

1. 熟读下列词组 Read the following phrases until you learn them by heart

（1）看得懂　听得懂　看得见　听得清楚　记得住　做得完　想得到

　　　看不懂　听不懂　看不见　听不清楚　记不住　做不完　想不到

　　　买得到　　唱得好　　学得会　　照得上

　　　买不到　　唱不好　　学不会　　照不上

（2）上得去　下得来　进得去　出得来　回得去　回得来　过得去　过得来

　　　上不去　下不来　进不去　出不来　回不去　回不来　过不去　过不来

（3）搬得出来　爬得上来　跳得过来　骑得回去　踢得进去　拿得上来

　　　开得进去　走不下去　游得过去　跑不回来　踢不进去　拿不上去

（4）想出来　　写出来　　看出来　　听出来　　回答出来

　　　想得出来　写得出来　看得出来　听得出来　回答得出来

　　　想不出来　写不出来　看不出来　听不出来　回答不出来

　　　感觉出来　　翻译出来

　　　感觉得出来　翻译得出来

　　　感觉不出来　翻译不出来

（5）人人　事事　家家　步步　年年　月月　日日　天天　次次

　　　张张照片　　个个学生　　个个生词　　件件事情　　篇篇文章

　　　间间住房　　座座大楼　　座座小山　　盆盆花儿　　场场比赛

　　　种种植物　　条条大街　　棵棵树　　本本书

　　　一年一年地　　一天一天地　　一步一步地　　一家一家地

　　　一个一个地　　一次一次地　　一棵一棵的　　一个一个的

　　　一盘一盘的　　一本一本的　　一张一张的　　一辆一辆的

2. 句型替换　Pattern drills

（1）A：他<u>看</u>得<u>懂</u> <u>这篇文章</u>吗？
　　　B：他<u>看</u>得<u>懂</u>。

看	见	山上的松树
听	懂	这个故事
借	到	那本小说
记	住	这么多的生词

（2）A：你<u>做</u>得<u>完</u> <u>做</u>不<u>完</u> <u>今天的练习</u>？
　　　B：我<u>做</u>不<u>完</u> <u>今天的练习</u>。

看	清楚	老师写的字
买	到	那种背包
办	完	这些事儿
找	到	他的自行车

（3）A：<u>汽车</u> <u>上</u>得来<u>上</u>不来？
　　　B：<u>这儿路不好</u>，<u>上</u>不来了。

小孩儿	下	他有点儿怕
你	回	我有很多事儿
她	过	人太多
大桌子	进	门太小

（4）A：<u>植树节的消息</u> <u>登</u>出来了没有？
　　　B：<u>植树节的消息</u> <u>登</u>出来了。

那篇文章	写
他要的这本书	找
书上的问题	回答
解决污染的办法	想

（5）A：现在大家都<u>关心</u>城市的<u>绿化</u>吗?

　　　B：现在<u>人人</u>都<u>关心</u>城市的<u>绿化</u>。

注意保护环境　　家家
认真锻炼身体　　人人
怕环境污染　　　个个

（6）A：他们正做什么呢?

　　　B：他们正<u>一步一步</u>地<u>往山上爬</u>呢。

一课一课　　复习生词
一盆一盆　　浇花儿
一间一间　　打扫宿舍

3. 课堂活动　Classroom activities

(1) One student says a word, and other students use the pattern "跟+N/Pr+有/没（有）关系" to make sentences. For example,

　　　A：纸

　　　B：纸是我自己买的，多用纸跟别人没关系。

　　　C：可是纸是木头做的，多用纸跟保护环境有关系。

　　　……　　　……

(2) One student says a word, and other students use the pattern "既……，又……" to make sentences. For example,

　　　A：公园

　　　B：在公园既能锻炼身体，又能看书。

　　　C：公园的环境既优美又安静。

　　　……　　　……

4. 会话练习 Conversation practice

> **会话常用语 IDIOMATIC EXPRESSIONS IN CONVERSATION**
>
> 你们可能不知道 (Perhaps you don't know...)
>
> 看得出来 (...one can tell/see (that)...; it is evident (that)...)
>
> 想不到 (it's unexpected (that)...)
>
> 跟……有关系 (be related to...)
>
> 你说得很对 (You are absolutely right.)

【表示可能 Indicating a possibility】

（1）A：今天中午你在餐厅见得到小张吗？

　　　B：我见得到他。有什么事儿？

　　　A：请你把这本书给他，好吗？

　　　B：没问题。

（2）A：咱们一起来照张相吧。这样站，行吗？

　　　B：力波，你得向宋华靠近一点儿，要不就照不上了。

（3）A：喂，大为在吗？

　　　B：哪位？请大点儿声，我听不清楚。

　　　A：听出来了吗？我是谁？

　　　B：对不起，我听不出来。

【表示担心 Expressing one's concern】

（1）A：你觉得这次足球赛的结果会怎样？

　　　B：怎么说呢？我们系足球队刚刚建立，说实在的，我有点儿担心。

　　　A：可不，我担心的是大宋可能不参加，他是队里技术最好的。

（2）A：这么晚了，他还没有回来。我担心他路上会不会出问题。

　　　B：是啊，他开车开得太快，真让人不放心。

【引起话题　Bringing up a topic】

（1）A：你们可能不知道，今年的夏令营不办了。

　　　B：是吗？真不巧，我朋友今年想参加夏令营。

（2）A：真想不到，今天会到31度。

　　　B：是啊，昨天还不到20度。

（3）A：对了，去植物园参观的事儿你告诉林娜了没有？

　　　B：我还没有找到她呢。我说，上次你借的那本书，看完了没有？

5. 看图说话 Describe the following pictures

❶ 搬……进去　搬……上来　　　❷ 跳……过去　爬……上去

6. 交际练习 Communication exercises

（1）While traveling in Guangzhou, someone speaks Cantonese to you. What would you say?

（2）Talk with your friends about something that you are worried about. After you speak, write down what you have said.

阅读与复述 Reading Comprehension and Paraphrasing

🎧28　熊猫（xióngmāo）是中国的国宝

　　熊猫又叫大熊猫，是中国特有的珍稀（zhēnxī）动物。它们只生活在中国西部的一些地方，那儿是2000米到4000米的高山和树林。因为环境的变化，熊猫已经越来越少了。中国人把熊猫叫做"国宝"，正在用各种办法抢救（qiǎngjiù）它。全世界的人也都喜欢它，关心它。中国已经给很多国家送去了熊猫。

　　以前在我们国家看不到大熊猫。中国野生动物保护协会（Zhōngguó Yěshēng Dòngwù Bǎohù Xiéhuì）决定（juédìng），要把大熊猫美美和田田送给我们国家的一个城市动物园（dòngwùyuán）。昨天我和一位中国朋友去北京动物园看这两只大熊猫。我们来到熊猫馆的时候，它们正在吃竹叶（zhú yè），样子既可爱，又可笑：胖（pàng）胖的身体，短短的腿（tuǐ）。头那么大，耳朵（ěrduo）那么小，眼睛像戴着墨镜（mòjìng）一样。它们不停地走过来走过去。有个小朋友大声地说："美美！田田！你们就要去外国了，让我给你们照张相吧！"美美和田田好像听懂了小朋友的话，它们站在竹子下边，看着那个小朋友，好像在问："我们这么站着，怎么样？你照得上吗？"

　　我问旁边的一个小姑娘："美美和田田就要坐飞机出国了，你以后就看不到它们了，你希望它们留（liú）在这儿吗？"

　　"当然希望它们留在这儿。可是，外国小朋友也很喜欢大熊猫，他们也都想早点儿看到美美和田田。"小姑娘非常认真地回答。

　　我看着美美和田田，看着这些可爱的小朋友，心里想，这两只可爱的大熊猫真是中国人民的友好使者（shǐzhě）啊。

三、语法 Grammar

1 可能补语（1） Complement of possibility (1)

"得/不" is inserted between a verb and a resultative or directional complement to indicate whether a result can be attained or a state can be achieved.

V ＋ 得 / 不 ＋ Resultative / Directional Complement

看	得		懂		(can understand after reading)
做		不	完		(cannot finish doing)
上	得			去	(can get on)
爬		不		上去	(cannot climb up to)

The affirmative-negative question for a sentence with a complement of possibility is "V+得+complement+V+不+complement". When the verb is followed by an object, the object is used after the complement of possibility. For example,

A: 你看得见看不见那个小木屋？

B: 小木屋在哪儿？我看不见。

A: 下午五点钟你回得来回不来？

B: 我回得来。

Notes:

❶ The negative form of the complement of possibility is more frequently used than the positive one. It indicates that the action cannot achieve a certain result or reach a certain state due to lack of certain subjective or objective condition(s). This meaning usually can only be expressed by using the complement of possibility, but not the optative verb. For example,

我只学了一年汉语，现在看不懂《红楼梦》。

(One cannot say: "我只学了一年汉语，现在不能看懂《红楼梦》。")

老师说得太快，我听不懂。

(One cannot say: "老师说得太快，我不能听懂。")

山很高，我爬不上去。

(One cannot say：“山很高，我不能爬上去。”)

他想了很长时间，想不出好办法来。

(One cannot say：“他想了很长时间，不能想出好办法来。”)

❷ The affirmative form of the complement of possibility is used less frequently. It is only used to ask or answer a question with a complement of possibility. For example,

> A：你坐在后边，听得清楚吗?
>
> B：我听得清楚。

② "出来"的引申用法　Extended usage of "出来"

The construction "V+出来" indicates that an action has given rise to something or some result. For example,

> 植树节的消息登出来了。
>
> 这个好主意是怎么想出来的?
>
> 他一定要写出一篇好文章来。
>
> 这个句子错了，你看得出来吗?

③ 名词、量词和数量词短语的重叠
The reduplication of nouns, measure words, and numeral-measure word phrases

Some reduplicated nouns and measure words denote "all" or "without exception". They are often used as subjects or attributive modifiers. For example,

> 现在人人都关心北京的绿化。
>
> 他们个个都喜欢用筷子。
>
> 件件衣服都小了。
>
> 篇篇文章都写得很好。

Note:

Reduplicated nouns and measure words cannot be used as the objects or attributive modifiers of the objects. For example, one cannot say: "我告诉人人。" "我喜欢张张照片。"

Reduplicated time words can be used as adverbials. For example,

他天天都打太极拳。

他去博物馆参观了很多次，次次都觉得很有意思。

Reduplicated numeral-measure word phrases, mainly the reduplicated pattern of "一+M", are used as adverbials that denote the manner of an action, meaning "one after another". It is followed by "地". For example,

我们一步一步地往上爬吧。(step by step)

他们的汉语水平正一天一天地提高。(day after day)

他一张一张地把照片给大家看。(one by one)

小学生排着队，两个两个地走进餐厅。(two by two)

Reduplicated numeral-measure word phrases used as attributive modifiers denote the description of something. It is followed by "的". For example,

一棵一棵的小树种得多整齐啊！

一盘一盘的水果放在桌子上。

一个一个的问题都回答对了。

4 既……，又……   The construction "既……，又……"

This structure is used to denote that two qualities or situations concurrently exist. For example,

在这里，学生们既能欣赏自然景色，又能接受保护环境的教育。

北京既是中国的首都，又是世界有名的大都市。

她既聪明又漂亮。

四、字与词 Chinese Characters and Words

构词法（7）：附加式 ①

Word formation method (7): Affixed compound words ①

The main character indicates the meaning of the word and the affixed character indicates the grammatical notion. The affixed compound words fall into two categories: the prefixed and the suffixed. For example,

"第" is prefixed to numerals to denote ordinal numbers, e.g. 第一，第二，第三，第十一.

"老" is prefixed to monosyllabic surnames to address acquaintances, e.g. 老张，老李.

Some words are also formed in this way, e.g. 老师，老板.

Famous Natural Scenic Spots in China

China is a country with rich tourism resources. By 2010, altogether 40 scenic spots and historical sites in China had been inscribed on the World Heritage List, including eight items of natural heritage and four items of both natural and cultural heritage. Among the numerous natural scenic spots, the most famous ones are as follows.

Wulingyuan Scenic Area, situated in Hunan Province, is best known for its quartz sandstone peak-forest landform with criss-cross ravines, countless streams, thick forests and wide varieties of terrestrial animals and plants. The strangely-shaped peaks, exotic stones, secluded valleys, clear waters and deep limestone caves form the "five wonders" of Wulingyuan and make it world-famous.

Jiuzhaigou Valley and Huanglong Scenic Area are both seated in Sichuan Province. Jiuzhaigou Valley (or Nine-Village Valley) is so named because there are nine Tibetan villages in the scenic area. It is reputed to be the "Fairy-tale World". Located 2,000–3,000 meters above sea level, the scenic area has a very pleasant climate, boasting the windless winter, cool summer and beautiful views all year round. Huanglong (literally "Yellow Dragon") Scenic Area is densely covered with calcium carbonate deposits and its terraced calcified waterfalls form an image like a giant golden dragon. With sceneries such as snow mountains, waterfalls, virgin forests and canyons and rare animals like giant pandas and golden monkeys, it is affectionately called the "World Wonder" and the "Fairy Land on Earth".

Shangri-La in Yunnan Province is known as the "Alpine Garden", "Kingdom of Animals and Plants" and "Kingdom of Nonferrous Metals". On this tranquil land, you can find holy snow mountains, fertile lands, flocks of cows and sheep, quiet lakes, divine temples and honest Khampa people as if you have walked into the paradise in your dream.

第三十四课
Lesson
34

神女峰的传说
The legend of Shennü Peak

When taking a boat tour of the Three Gorges, Ma Dawei felt slightly dizzy and lost his appetite. Xiao Yanzi took good care of him. The next day, either because he had a sound sleep last night, or Xiao Yanzi's care, Ma Dawei felt better and was able to enjoy the scenery of the Shennü Peak.

一、课文 Text

29 (一)

小燕子：大为，吃饭了。

马大为：我站起来就头晕，不想吃。再说，船上的菜个个都辣，^① 我可吃不下去。^②

补充说明

Making additional remarks

小燕子：前几天，四川菜你吃得很高兴啊！而且，你还讲过一个故事：有三个人比赛吃辣的，一个是四川人，他说不怕辣；一个是湖北人，他说辣不怕；一个是湖南人，他说怕不辣。你说你是怕不辣的，今天怎么又说四川菜太辣？^③ 是不是晕船啊？

马大为：不知道。

小燕子：喝点儿可乐吧。

马大为：这可乐的味儿也不对了。好像也有辣味儿了，跟我在美国喝

　　　　的不一样。

小燕子：可乐哪儿来的辣味儿？

马大为：我不想喝。这儿连空气都有辣味儿，

　　　　我觉得全身都不舒服。

小燕子：晕船的药你吃了没有？④

马大为：晕船的药我带来了，可是没找着。我不记得放在哪儿了。

小燕子：没关系，我到医务室去，给你要点儿。

马大为：谢谢。

　　　　……

小燕子：晕船药要来了。你把它吃下去，一会儿就好了。

马大为：刚才我睡着了。船开到哪儿了？好像停住了。外边安静得听

　　　　不见一点儿声音。我想出去看看。

小燕子：你可别出去。刮风了，外边有点儿凉。你应该吃点儿什么。

马大为：我头晕好点儿了，不过，还不想吃东西，就想睡觉。

小燕子：那你就再睡一会儿吧。快到三峡的时候，我一定叫你。

生词 New Words

1. 传说	chuánshuō	N	legend	三峡的传说，神女峰的传说
2. 晕	yūn	V	to feel dizzy	头晕，觉得头晕，有点儿晕

3. 再说	zàishuō	Conj	what's more
4. 船	chuán	N	boat, ship　坐船，上船，开船，在船上，船上的菜
5. 辣	là	A	hot, spicy　辣的菜，不辣的菜，喜欢辣，个个都辣
6. 可	kě	Adv	*used for emphasis*　我可吃不下去，你可别出去
7. 讲	jiǎng	V	to tell, to explain, to speak　讲故事，讲课文，讲生词，讲语法，讲话
8. 怕	pà	V	to fear, to be afraid of　怕小偷，怕发烧，怕头晕，怕坐船，怕考试，怕麻烦，怕脏，不怕辣，怕不辣
9. 晕船	yùnchuán	VO	to feel sick because of the movement of a boat or ship　怕晕船，有点儿晕船，晕船药
10. 可乐	kělè	N	coke or soft drink similar to Coca-Cola　喝点儿可乐
11. 味儿	wèir	N	taste, flavor　辣味儿，可乐的味儿，菜的味儿
12. 连	lián	Conj	even　连空气也有辣味儿
13. 着	zháo	V	*used after a verb as a complement to indicate the result of the action*　睡着，睡不着，找着，买不着
14. 医务室	yīwùshì	N	clinic　学校医务室
15. 刮	guā	V	to blow　刮风
16. 凉	liáng	A	cool, cold　外边有点儿凉，天气很凉，水有点儿凉，菜凉了，凉水
17. 神女峰	Shénnǚ Fēng	PN	Shennü Peak
18. 四川	Sìchuān	PN	a province in southwest China with its capital in Chengdu

19. 湖北	Húběi	PN	a province in central China with its capital in Wuhan
20. 湖南	Húnán	PN	a province of China in the south of the middle reaches of the Yangtze River with its capital in Changsha
21. 三峡	Sānxiá	PN	the Three Gorges (of the Yangtze River)

注释　Notes

① 再说，船上的菜个个都辣。

"Besides, every dish cooked on the ship is spicy."

The conjunction "再说" connects clauses to make further explanation. It may be followed by a pause. For example,

丁力波明天不去长城，他已经去过了。再说，他明天还有别的事儿。

我不太喜欢这个戏，故事太一般了。再说，几个主要角色也演得不太自然。

The conjunction "而且" also functions the same way. For example,

四川菜你吃得很高兴啊！而且，你还讲过一个故事。

② 我可吃不下去。

"I just cannot eat any more."

The adverb "可" is used before a verb or an adjective to make emphasis. It's mainly used in spoken Chinese. For example,

我可知道他的意思，他不愿意来。

快考试了，可不能再看电视了。

外边可热闹了。

这件事儿可不简单。

③ 你说你是怕不辣的，今天怎么又说四川菜太辣？

"You said that you were worried that the food was not hot enough, but today, why are you saying that the Sichuan dishes are too hot?"

The adverb "又" (4) expresses a transition between two contradictory situations. The conjunction "可是" may be placed before it. For example,

她很怕冷，又不愿意多穿衣服。

他刚才说要参加聚会，现在又说不参加了。

我很想把这件事儿告诉你，可是又担心你听了会不高兴。

④ 晕船的药你吃了没有？

"Did you take the medicine for sickness?"

In spoken Chinese, "晕船（的）药" refers to "the medicine for sickness". Other examples include "感冒药，头疼的药".

🎧 30 （二）

小燕子：快起来，我们去看日出。

马大为：你先去吧。我把咖啡喝了就去。

小燕子：你今天好点儿了吧？昨天还没有到神女峰呢，就被神女迷住了，晕得连可乐也不想喝了。

马大为：别提了，昨天我是晕了。⑤ 既有美丽的神女，又有从早到晚为我忙的小燕子，你们把我迷住了。

小燕子：你又来了。⑥

马大为：三峡实在是太美了！李白的一首诗我记住了两句："两岸猿声啼不住，轻舟已过万重山。"

小燕子：我看应该说"大为头晕止不住，游船已过万重山"。

马大为：小燕子，你又开玩笑了。我们一起来欣赏三峡景色吧。

小燕子：三峡有很多传说，最感人的是神女峰的传说。

叙述
Telling a story

马大为：你说说。

小燕子：神女峰是三峡最有名、最美的山峰。很久很久以前，西王母让她美丽的女儿来三峡，为来往的大船小船指路。⑦ 她日日夜夜地站在那儿，后来就成了神女峰。

马大为：三峡的景色真像是一幅中国山水画。坐船游三峡，真是"船在水中走，人在画中游"。

小燕子：你看，前面就是世界第一大坝——三峡大坝，多壮观啊！

生词 New Words

1.	日出	rì chū		sunrise	日出，看日出
2.	迷	mí	V	to be fascinated	迷住，被美丽的景色迷住了，球迷，京剧迷
3.	为	wèi	Prep	for	为公司工作，为我忙，为他担心，为友谊干杯
4.	首	shǒu	M	a measure word for poems and songs, etc.	一首歌
5.	诗	shī	N	poem	古诗，唐诗，一首诗

6. 两岸猿声啼不住	Liǎng àn yuán shēng tí bú zhù		the monkeys on both banks are still gibbering
7. 轻舟已过万重山	Qīng zhōu yǐ guò wàn chóng shān		the boat has flown away past tens of thousands of hills
8. 止	zhǐ	V	to stop　止住，止不住
9. 游船	yóuchuán	N	pleasure boat　坐游船
10. 久	jiǔ	A	long (time)　很久以前，好久不见，有多久
11. 来往	láiwǎng	V	to come and go　来往的船，来往的火车，来往的乘客
12. 指	zhǐ	V	to point at　指路
13. 夜	yè	N	night　夜里，日日夜夜
14. 山水画	shānshuǐhuà	N	landscape painting　中国山水画，像一幅山水画
山水	shānshuǐ	N	mountain and water, landscape
15. 坝	bà	N	dam　大坝，三峡大坝
16. 壮观	zhuàngguān	A	grand, spectacular, magnificent
17. 李白	Lǐ Bái	PN	Li Bai (name of a great Chinese poet of the Tang Dynasty)
18. 西王母	Xīwángmǔ	PN	Queen Mother of the West (a figure in Chinese mythology)

补充生词 Supplementary Words

1. 血	xiě	N	blood
2. 果树	guǒshù	N	fruit tree
3. 打鱼	dǎ yú	V O	to go fishing
4. 掉	diào	V	to fall

5.	张学良	Zhāng Xuéliáng	PN	Zhang Xueliang (name of a well-known Chinese general of the 1930s)
6.	鼻烟壶	bíyānhú	N	snuff bottle
7.	工艺品	gōngyìpǐn	N	handicraft product
8.	透明	tòumíng	A	transparent
9.	珍贵	zhēnguì	A	valuable, precious
10.	收藏	shōucáng	V	to collect
11.	将军服	jiāngjūnfú	N	general's uniform
	将军	jiāngjūn	N	general
12.	画像	huàxiàng	N	portrait
13.	夏威夷	Xiàwēiyí	PN	Hawaii
14.	轮椅	lúnyǐ	N	wheelchair
15.	握	wò	V	to hold
16.	缘分	yuánfèn	N	predestined opportunity for people to be brought together
17.	微笑	wēixiào	V	to smile

注释　Notes

⑤ 别提了，昨天我是晕了。

"Don't talk about it again. I was dizzy yesterday."

Here, "别提了" means "do not talk about that matter again". It often refers to something unpleasant that the speaker does not want to talk about any more. For example，

别提了，这场球踢得真糟糕。

别提了，那场音乐会水平低极了。

⑥ 你又来了。

"Here you come again."

This expression is used when the speaker is unsatisfied about what the other party said or did again. It is often used between acquaintances. In the text, Xiao Yanzi means "you are saying those flattering words again".

⑦ 为来往的大船小船指路。

"To navigate the coming and going ships."

"为+Pr/N" functions as an adverbial to introduce the recipient of an action. For example,

小燕子从早到晚为我忙。

他每天都为大家服务。

The prepositional phrase "为+NP/VP" is also used to denote a reason or purpose. For example,

我们都为这件事着急。

为我们的友谊，干杯!

为养好盆景，他买了很多书。

二、练习 Exercises

练习与运用 Drills and Practice 31

核心句 KEY SENTENCES

1. 我可吃不下去。
2. 你说你是怕不辣的，今天怎么又说四川菜太辣?
3. 晕船的药你吃了没有?
4. 刚才我睡着了。
5. 刮风了!
6. 晕得连可乐也不想喝了。
7. 李白的一首诗我记住了两句。
8. 她为来往的大船小船指路。

1. 熟读下列词组　Read the following phrases until you learn them by heart

（1）拿住　　站住　　停住　　抓住　　止住　　记住　　关住　　迷住
　　　拿得住　站得住　停得住　抓得住　止得住　记得住　关得住　迷得住
　　　拿不住　站不住　停不住　抓不住　止不住　记不住　关不住　迷不住

（2）找着　　借着　　打着　　睡着　　买着　　见着　　等着　　抓着
　　　找得着　借得着　打得着　睡得着　买得着　见得着　等得着　抓得着
　　　找不着　借不着　打不着　睡不着　买不着　见不着　等不着　抓不着

（3）为我们忙　　　为大家服务　　为大学生演奏　　　为你的成绩高兴
　　　为女儿担心　　为结业聚会　　为这件事情着急　　为我们的友谊干杯

（4）可喜欢了　可了解了　可尊重了　可不能问　可不想去　可别出去
　　　可冷了　　可忙了　　可远了　　可高兴了　可热闹了　可认真了
　　　可倒霉了　可不简单　可不谦虚

（5）刮风了　　下雨了　　下雪了　　上课了　　下课了　　上班了
　　　吃饭了　　起床了　　到站了

2. 句型替换　Pattern drills

（1）A：晕船的药你吃了吗?
　　　B：晕船的药我吃了。

可乐	买来了
医务室	去了
船票	买得到
三峡的日出	看过

（2）A：四川菜他吃得怎么样?
　　　B：四川菜他吃得很高兴。

这次考试	准备	很认真
第34课语法	讲	很清楚
这次活动	搞	还可以
环境保护问题	研究	很好

（3）A：那本书你找着了没有？

　　B：那本书我没找着。

　　A：你还找得着吗？

　　B：我看，我找不着了。

那个生词	查
到上海的火车票	买
那位女科学家	见
张教授要的房子	租

（4）A：船 停住了没有？

　　B：船 停住了。

前边的人	站
偷她钱的小偷	抓
胳膊上的血 (xiě)	止
这首诗	记

（5）A：这儿怎么样？

　　B：这儿很安静，连一点儿声音也没有。

热闹	舞厅	都有
不方便	一个商店	也没有
方便	邮局	都有
热	一点儿风	也没有

（6）A：你看得懂英文小说吗？

　　B：看不懂，我连一句英文也没有学过。

会书法	不会	汉字	写不好
认识小燕子	不认识	这个名字	没有听说过
参观过兵马俑	没有	西安	没去过
常去网吧	没去过	电脑	不会用

（7）大家都为<u>他高兴</u>。

环境污染　　担心
等公共汽车　着急
生病的同学　做了很多事儿
知识大赛　　作准备

（8）A：咱们<u>喝点儿什么</u>吧。
　　　B：好吧。

去哪儿玩儿玩儿
找谁问问路
请谁帮一下
什么时候去看看老师

3. 课堂活动　Classroom activity

A student says a sentence. Another student uses "又" to express a transition and the opposite situation. For example，

A：明天我想去长城，

B：又怕会下雨。

C：又想在学校看球赛。

……　　……

4. 会话练习　Conversation practice

会话常用语 IDIOMATIC EXPRESSIONS IN CONVERSATION

一会儿就好了 (I will be fine in a minute.)

别提了 (Don't talk about it again.)

你又来了 (Here you come again.)

很久很久以前 (Long long ago)

【补充说明　Making additional remarks】

A：春节你打算去旅游吗？

B：天气太冷，我不想去。再说，我还得打工，挣点儿钱。

A：冬天旅游是差点儿。可是，我已经买好了游三峡的船票，而且我还跟我朋友说好了，我们一起去。

【表示强调　Making emphasis】

A：你们家来的电话吧？你们那儿现在情况怎么样？

B：这几年，我们那儿变化可大了。我们家虽然在农村，可是人们的生活跟城里人差不多。现在家家都有电视、电话什么的。有的人还买了汽车，他们卖蔬菜、水果都用汽车送。连小孩儿上中学也不用到城里去了，我们村有中学，也有医院了。

A：你们那儿是发展得很快。我们家那儿，农民的生活水平还很低，农民挣钱可不容易了，有的连孩子上小学都有问题。不过，现在很多技术人员去我们那儿帮助农民种果树（guǒshù）。再过几年，农民的生活一定会好一些。

【叙述　Telling a story】

A：神女峰的传说可不少，我再给你们讲一个，怎么样？

B：好啊。

A：很久很久以前，在这个山顶上住着一对年轻的丈夫和妻子。丈夫每天都去江里打鱼（dǎ yú），妻子在家里做饭、洗衣服。妻子每天做好晚饭以后，就站在山顶上看着江水，等着丈夫回来。一天，丈夫又到长江里打鱼去了。到了晚上，丈夫还没有回来。这时候，刮起了大风，下起了大雨。小船被撞坏了，丈夫掉（diào）到了江里。他妻子在家里不见他回来，非常着急，就爬到山顶上，看着江水，等他回家。

B：后来呢？

A：后来时间一天一天地、一年一年地过去了，她丈夫到现在也没有

回来，她还在那儿等着。

B：哦，这个神女看着江水，还真像那位年轻的妻子在等她的丈夫。

5. 看图说话　Describe the following pictures

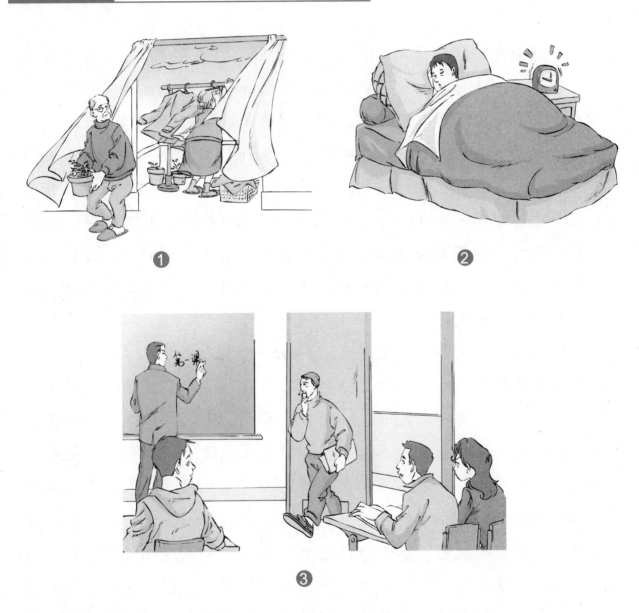

6. 交际练习　Communication exercises

Tell one of your favorite legends or stories. After you speak, write down what you have said.

阅读与复述 Reading Comprehension and Paraphrasing

🎧 32 张学良（Zhāng Xuéliáng）的鼻烟壶（bíyānhú）

鼻烟壶是中国传统的工艺品（gōngyìpǐn），已经有200多年的历史了。它是用一种特别的画笔，在透明（tòumíng）的鼻烟壶里画画儿。有名的工艺美术家画的鼻烟壶，是很珍贵（zhēnguì）的艺术品。

张学良先生最大的爱好是收藏（shōucáng）鼻烟壶。1992年，他收到了一份让他感到惊奇的礼物。那是一个鼻烟壶，鼻烟壶里画了张学良年轻时穿着将军服（jiāngjūnfú）的画像（huàxiàng）。张先生得到这份珍贵的礼物，非常高兴，把它放在床边的小桌上时时欣赏。他以为这一定是一位很有经验的老画家的作品。因为现在能在鼻烟壶内作画儿的人已经越来越少了。

1998年，中国在美国夏威夷（Xiàwēiyí）举办工艺美术展览。每天来参观展览的人很多。当时，张将军已经快一百岁了，他听说展品中有鼻烟壶，就坐着轮椅（lúnyǐ）来参观展览。张先生没有想到的是，那位为他画像的工艺美术家也来了。张先生更没有想到的是，他会是一位这么年轻的艺术家。张先生热情地握（wò）住年轻人的手，很高兴地对他说："我今天能在这儿见到你，真是缘分（yuánfèn）啊！缘分啊！"这位年轻艺术家告诉张先生，他为了完成这幅作品，到北京图书馆查了很多书，看了不少有关张将军的图片。张先生和张夫人感到非常高兴，他们跟这位年轻的艺术家一起照了相。在照片上，这位百岁老人正向我们微笑（wēixiào）呢！

三、语法　Grammar

1 主谓谓语句（2）Sentences with a subject-predicate phrase as predicate (2)

In a sentence with a subject-predicate phrase as predicate, the subject of the whole sentence (Subject$_1$) is the receiver of the action denoted by the predicate (Predicate$_2$) in the subject-predicate phrase, which acts as the predicate of the whole sentence (Predicate$_1$).

Subject$_1$	Predicate$_1$	
	Subject$_2$	Predicate$_2$
晕船的药	你	吃了没有？
新汉语词典	同学们	都 买到了。
张教授讲的课	我	现在还 听不懂。
四川菜	你	吃得很高兴啊！
这儿的风俗习惯	他	了解得很多。

Although the subject is the receiver of the action in the sentence, it is what the whole sentence is about. Compare the following:

晕船的药我吃了。（晕船的药呢？晕船的药怎么样？）

我吃晕船的药了。（你做什么了？你怎么样？）

2 疑问代词表示虚指　Interrogative pronouns indicating indefinite reference

Besides forming questions or rhetorical questions, interrogative pronouns can also be used to denote somebody, something, some time, some place, or manner that is unknown or uncertain to the speaker, or that the speaker is unable or unwilling to tell. For example,

你应该吃点儿什么。

我不记得放在哪儿了。

这件事儿好像谁告诉过我。

我不知道怎么扭了一下胳膊。

3 "着 (zháo)、住" 做结果补语　"着" and "住" as the resultative complements

The construction "V+着" is used to indicate that certain goal or result of an action has been achieved. For example,

晕船的药我没找着。

他要的那本书我借着了。

刚才我睡着了。

"V+住" is used to indicate that the position of somebody or something has been stabilized through an action. For example,

船好像停住了。

请站住。

小偷被抓住了。

李白的一首诗我记住了两句。

A verb and the resultative complement "着" or "住" can also form a complement of possibility. For example, 找得着, 睡不着, 记不住, 止不住.

4　无主句　The subjectless sentence

Some Chinese sentences do not have subjects in the real sense. Most of them consist of a verb-object phrase and generally describe natural phenomena. For example,

下雨了。

下雪了。

刮风了。

Some of these sentences indicate the emergence of a new situation. For example,

上课了，请大家不要说话了。

吃饭了，咱们先复习到这儿。

5　连X也/都……　The construction "连X也/都……"

The structure "连X也/都……" is used for emphasis. "X" is the emphasized part placed after the preposition "连". The adverb "也" or "都" follows the emphasized part. This structure is used to indicate a comparison: "even X is this way, let alone others". For example,

这儿连空气都有辣味儿。　　　　　　　　（个个菜都是辣的）

他晕得连可乐也不想喝了。　　　　　　　（别的事儿更不想做了）

他连吃药、喝水都要别人帮助，病得不轻。（他更不能起床，不能上班）

我连他姓什么也不知道。　　　　　　　　（我不了解他）

四、字与词　Chinese Characters and Words

构词法（8）：附加式 ②

Word formation method (8): Affixed compound words ②

An affix is attached after a single or a compound word to form a new word.

(1) "子" is attached after other words to form nouns. For example,

刀子　叉子　杯子　盘子　筷子　瓶子　桌子　妻子

儿子　孙子　孩子　房子　嗓子　本子　样子　小伙子

(2) "儿" (not a syllable itself) is attached after other words to form nouns. For example, 花儿, 画儿, 点儿, 事儿.

"儿" can also be attached to a few specific verbs to form a retroflex ending. For example, 玩儿.

Note: "子" and "儿" are read in the neutral tone. When they do not function as suffixes, they are not read in the neutral tone. For example, 孔子, 男子, 女儿.

(3) "者" is attached after some verbs to form nouns. For example, 记者, 作者, 译者, 读者, 爱好者, 工作者, 学习者.

(4) "化" is attached after some adjectives or nouns to form verbs. For example, 绿化, 科学化.

(5) "家" is attached after some nouns or verbs to form nouns. For example, 文学家, 科学家, 艺术家, 画家.

Famous Mountains in China

China is home to numerous famous mountains, which all have their distinctive features. Some of them are mighty, some are strangely-shaped, and others are mysterious and beautiful.

When it comes to famous mountains, people always bring up the Five Sacred Mountains. They are respectively Mount Tai in the east (in Shandong Province), Mount Hua in the west (in Shaanxi Province), Mount Heng in the north (in Shanxi Province), Mount Heng in the south (in Hunan Province) and Mount Song in the middle (in Henan Province), among which Mount Tai is the most revered. Located in the eastern part of China, Mount Tai is a historical mountain on which emperors of different dynasties and many celebrities had left their footprints as well as a large number of cultural relics. Therefore, it has been inscribed on the UNESCO World Heritage List as a cultural and natural heritage site.

Then there are the top four mountains for tourism, the most famous one being Huangshan Mountain in Anhui Province, which we have already mentioned in the text of Lesson 31. Xu Xiake, a noted traveler of the Ming Dynasty, wrote the famous line that "Having visited the Sacred Mountain in the east, one does not care to see other mountains; and having visited Huangshan Mountain, one does not care to see the Sacred Mountains". Lushan Mountain in Jiangxi Province is famous for its summer resorts and historical celebrities there. Wuyi Mountain in Fujian Province is said to have the "best scenery in southeast China", with unique green water and red mountain which enjoy a high reputation. Yandang Mountain in Zhejiang Province is known at home and abroad as "a resort with unrivaled beauty" and the "No.1 Mountain in southeast China".

Besides, there are also many famous mountains in China which are closely related to religions. For instance, there are the Four Taoist Mountains including Wudang Mountain in Hubei Province, Qingcheng Mountain in Sichuan Province, Dragon and Tiger Mountain in Jiangxi Province and Qiyun Mountain in Anhui Province, and the Four Buddhist Mountains, which are Putuo Mountain in Zhejiang Province, Wutai Mountain in Shanxi Province, Emei Mountain in Sichuan Province and Jiuhua Mountain in Anhui Province.

第三十五课

Lesson 35

汽车我先开着

Let me drive the car first.

Wang Xiaoyun is talking with her mother about buying a car. They have an argument because they have different ideas on consumption. This lesson will reveal the generation gap between them.

一、课文 Text

🎧 33 （一）

王小云：妈，开始工作以后，我就要买
汽车。

母　亲：什么？你现在还没开始工作，
就想买汽车的事儿？真不知道
你每天都在想些什么。

王小云：这跟工作没关系。

母　亲：怎么没关系？年轻人骑着自行
车上班，不是挺好的吗？既锻
炼了身体，又节约了钱。你爸
爸一辈子都这样。为什么你就
不能向你爸爸学习呢？

责备与质问
**Reproaching and
questioning**

王小云：都21世纪了，还骑自行车上班！① 自己开车多方便，想去哪
儿就去哪儿！再说，开车最少比骑车快一倍，可以节约二分之
一的时间。您知道吗？时间就是生命，时间就是金钱。

母　亲：就是21世纪，生活也得艰苦朴素，也得勤俭过日子。

王小云：大家都艰苦朴素，国家生产的汽车怎么办？都让它们在那儿
摆着？经济怎么发展？

母　亲：买汽车是有钱人的事儿。②我和你爸爸都没钱，你什么时候

　　　　挣够了钱，什么时候再买汽车。

王小云：您别管，我自己会想办法。

母　亲：你还能想出什么办法来？告诉你，你可别想着我们的那点儿

　　　　钱啊。那是我和你爸爸一辈子的积蓄。

王小云：您放心吧，您的钱我一分也不要。我想好了，等我工作以

　　　　后，我就去向银行贷款。③

母　亲：贷款买车？你疯了！

王小云：妈，现在贷款买车的人越来越多了。

生词 New Words

1. 挺	tǐng	Adv	(*coll.*) very, quite	挺好，挺辣，挺清楚，挺自然
2. 节约	jiéyuē	V	to save, to economize	节约钱，节约水，节约纸，节约时间
3. 一辈子	yíbèizi	N	all one's life, one's lifetime	一辈子谦虚，一辈子辛苦，一辈子都这样，工作了一辈子，研究了一辈子
4. 世纪	shìjì	N	century	21世纪，上个世纪，下半个世纪，新世纪
5. 倍	bèi	M	time, fold	一倍，快一倍，多两倍，提高三倍
6. ……分之……	……fēn zhī……		*used to express a fraction, percentage*	二分之一，五分之二，百分之二十

7. 就是	jiùshì	Conj	*used for emphasis*
8. 生命	shēngmìng	N	life 人的生命，时间就是生命
9. 金钱	jīnqián	N	money 节约金钱，时间就是金钱
金（子）	jīn (zi)	N	gold
10. 艰苦	jiānkǔ	A	arduous, hard 艰苦的生活，艰苦的工作
11. 朴素	pǔsù	A	simple, plain 艰苦朴素，朴素的衣服，生活很朴素
12. 勤俭	qínjiǎn	A	hard-working and thrifty 勤俭地生活
13. 日子	rìzi	N	day, life 过日子，勤俭过日子，好日子
14. 生产	shēngchǎn	V	to produce 生产汽车，生产咖啡，生产西装，汽车生产，提高生产
15. 经济	jīngjì	N	economy 国家经济，世界经济，发展经济
16. 管	guǎn	V	to bother about, to mind 你别管我的事儿，我不管这件事儿
17. 积蓄	jīxù	N/V	savings; to save 有点儿积蓄，一辈子的积蓄；积蓄力量
18. 贷款	dàikuǎn	VO/N	to provide or to ask for a loan; loan 向银行贷款；一笔贷款，还贷款
贷	dài	V	to borrow or to lend 借贷，贷一笔款
款	kuǎn	N	money 借款，还款，车款，房款
19. 疯	fēng	V	to be mad, to be crazy 你疯了，发疯

注释　Notes

① 都21世纪了，还骑自行车上班！

"(It's) already the twenty-first century. Still going to work by bike?"

In spoken Chinese, the adverb "都" is used to indicate "已经". For example,

你都借钱过日子了，还不丢人？

都十一点半了，他还不睡觉。

② 买汽车是有钱人的事儿。

　　"Only the rich can afford a car."

　　"有钱人" means "the rich".

③ 等我工作以后，我就去向银行贷款。

　　"After I find a job, I will apply for a loan from a bank."

The pattern "等+VP/S–PP（+的时候/以后）" is used before the main clause to indicate the time when the action in the main clause takes place. "等" suggests that there is still some time before it. In the main clause, we often use words like "就、再、才". For example,

　　等吃了饭，咱们就走。

　　等回国以后，我就去看她。

　　等他上班的时候你们再去找他。

　　等我打完电话，才发现陈老师已经走了。

34 （二）

母　亲：贷款不就是借债吗？你为买车借债？这就是你想的好办法？

王小云：对啊！

母　亲：我告诉你，不行！绝对不行！

拒绝
Refusing

王小云：为什么不行呢？

母　亲：我这辈子一次债都没有借过。就是过去困难的时候没钱买米，我也不借债。你不能给我丢人。④

王小云：我向银行贷款，按时还钱，这怎么是丢人呢？

母　亲：你都借钱过日子了，还不丢人？再说，银行怎么会借给你钱？

王小云：这您就不了解了。您以为谁想借银行的钱谁就能借到？银行的钱只借给两种人……

母　亲：哪两种人？

王小云：一种是有钱人……

母　亲：你说什么？有钱人还借债？

王小云：对。另一种是有信用的人。

母　亲：你不能算第一种人吧？

王小云：对，我不是第一种人，可我是第二种人。⑤

母　亲：你有"信用"？你的"信用"在哪儿？

王小云：您听我说，我工作以后，有了稳定的

解释
Making an explanation

收入，这就开始有了信用。我先付车款的十分之一或者五分之一，其余的向银行贷款。汽车我先开着，贷款我慢慢地还着。每年还百分之十或二十，几年以后，我把钱还完了，车就是我的了。我先借了钱，又按时还了钱，我的信用也就越来越高了。那时候，我又该换新车

了。我再向银行借更多的钱，买更好的车。我不但要借钱买

车，而且还要借钱买房子，借钱去旅游，借钱……

母　亲：这叫提高信用啊？我看，你在说梦话。

王小云：您不知道。在商品经济时代，信用就是这样建立的。跟您这

么说吧，一辈子不借钱的人……

母　亲：我认为他最有信用！

王小云：不对。他一点儿"信用"也没有！妈，您老的观念跟不上

时代了，⑥得变一变了。您要学会花明天的钱，实现今天的

梦。这对国家、对个人都有好处。

母　亲：你爱怎么做就怎么做，我不管。让我借债来享受生活，我做

不到。

生词 New Words

1. 借债	jièzhài	VO	to borrow money　向他借债
债	zhài	N	debt　还债
2. 绝对	juéduì	Adv	absolutely　绝对不行，绝对可以，绝对干净，绝对不会，绝对没有
3. 困难	kùnnan	A/N	difficult; difficulty　困难的时候，困难的日子，困难的问题；有困难，不怕困难
*4. 米	mǐ	N	rice　用米做饭，没有钱买米
5. 丢人	diūrén	VO	to lose face, to be disgraced　给我丢人，真丢人，丢人的事儿

6.	按时	ànshí	Adv	timely, on time 按时还钱，按时还书，按时交钱，按时交练习，按时复习
7.	信用	xìnyòng	N	credit 有信用，没有信用，建立信用，提高信用
8.	稳定	wěndìng	A	stable 稳定的收入，稳定的生活，稳定的关系
9.	付	fù	V	to pay 付款，付车款，付钱
10.	其余	qíyú	Pr	the remainder, the rest 其余的人，其余的贷款，其余的债
11.	梦话	mènghuà	N	words uttered in one's sleep, nonsense 说梦话
	梦	mèng	N	dream 做梦，今天的梦
12.	商品经济	shāngpǐn jīngjì		commodity economy
	商品	shāngpǐn	N	commodity, goods 商品很多，商品生产
13.	跟	gēn	V	to follow 跟谁，跟得上，跟不上他
14.	时代	shídài	N	times, era 新时代，商品经济时代，跟得上时代
15.	观念	guānniàn	N	concept 新观念，旧观念，老观念
16.	变	biàn	V	to change 观念变了，看法变了，主意变了，习惯变了，方式变了，天气变了，时代变了，意思变了
17.	实现	shíxiàn	V	to realize 实现今天的梦，实现理想
18.	好处	hǎochu	N	benefit 有好处，没有好处，对国家有好处
19.	享受	xiǎngshòu	V	to enjoy 享受生活，懂得享受

补充生词 Supplementary Words

| 1. | 高薪 | gāoxīn | N | high salary |

2.	穷人	qióngrén	N	the poor
3.	乱	luàn	A	at random, at will
4.	消费	xiāofèi	V	to consume
5.	追求	zhuīqiú	V	to pursue
6.	大部分	dà bùfen		majority
7.	存款	cúnkuǎn	N/VO	bank savings; to deposit money
8.	交际	jiāojì	V	to communicate
9.	今朝有酒	jīn zhāo yǒu jiǔ		"Get drunk while there is still wine";
	今朝醉	jīn zhāo zuì		to indulge oneself for the moment without caring about the future
10.	奋斗	fèndòu	V	to struggle, to strive
11.	美德	měidé	N	virtue

注释　Notes

④ 你不能给我丢人。

   "Don't disgrace me like that."

   The verb "给" means "to let, to make". It is used in the same way as "叫" and "让". We may also say "你不能让我丢人". "给" is frequently used in spoken Chinese.

⑤ 对，我不是第一种人，可我是第二种人。

   "Right. I am not the first type, but I am the second."

   Here, "可" means "可是".

⑥ 您老的观念跟不上时代了。

   "Your views are behind the times."

   The character "老" is used after "您" or a surname to show respect. "您老" is generally used to address the elderly, and "老" is used after a surname to address an old person who is erudite or has a high social status. For example, 张老, 王老.

二、练习 Exercises

练习 与运用 Drills and Practice 35

核心句 KEY SENTENCES

1. 我想去哪儿就去哪儿!
2. 开车最少比骑车快一倍,可以节约二分之一的时间。
3. 你什么时候挣够了钱,什么时候再买汽车。
4. 您的钱我一分也不要。
5. 等我工作以后,我就去向银行贷款。
6. 就是过去困难的时候没钱买米,我也不借债。
7. 你都借钱过日子了,还不丢人?
8. 您以为谁想借银行的钱谁就能借到?
9. 他一点儿"信用"也没有!
10. 你爱怎么做就怎么做。

1. 熟读下列词组 Read the following phrases until you learn them by heart

（1）快一倍　　贵两倍　　大五倍　　多十倍

车款的十分之一　　　　房款的五分之四

还了贷款的百分之十　　节约了二分之一的时间

（2）都21世纪了　都20岁了　都11点了　都两年了　都看过三遍了

（3）等我有空儿的时候　　等中秋节的时候　　　等我工作以后

等他有了房子以后　　等雨停了以后

（4）哪儿好玩儿就去哪儿　　　　喜欢住哪儿就住哪儿

在哪儿上班就在哪儿休息　　我走到哪儿小狗就跟到哪儿

什么便宜就买什么　　　　　什么时候方便就什么时候来

想说什么就说什么　　愿意给谁就给谁　　　喜欢谁就送给谁
谁的东西谁就拿走　　谁想参加谁就参加　　怎么教就怎么学
想怎么吃就怎么吃　　愿意怎么写就怎么写　他怎么问你就怎么回答

2. 句型替换　Pattern drills

（1）A：你什么时候买车?

　　　B：什么时候挣够了钱就什么时候买车。

我	去找他	你有时间
我们	吃饭	做好饭
他们	买房子	能向银行贷款

（2）A：咱们去哪儿?

　　　B：你想去哪儿就去哪儿!

买点儿什么	什么便宜就买什么。
送她什么礼物	她喜欢什么礼物就送她什么礼物。
让谁演主角	谁演得好就让谁演。
怎么去剧场	怎么方便就怎么去。
买多少纸	你要用多少就买多少。

（3）A：他有没有信用?

　　　B：他一点儿信用也没有!

王老师	时间	一点儿
他	丝绸衬衫	一件
她	中文古书	一本
夏令营	书法爱好者	一个
这个越剧团里	男演员	一个

（4）A：这些传说你听说过吗？

　　　B：这些传说我一个也没 听说过。

油画	喜欢	一幅也不
辣的菜	想吃	一个也不
问题	研究过	一个也没
事儿	知道	一点儿也不

（5）A：你向别人借过债吗？

　　　B：没有。就是没钱买米我也不向别人借债。

明天参加植树	参加	别人都不参加	要参加
想学中国画	想	有很大困难	要学
管过你的弟弟妹妹	没有	他们让我管	不管
认为现在要艰苦朴素	要	我很有钱	要艰苦朴素

（6）A：这两辆汽车哪辆 贵？

　　　B：这辆汽车比那辆贵 一倍。

（条）河	长	两倍
（间）房子	大	三分之一
（棵）树	高	五分之二
（个）学校的学生	多	百分之三十

（7）A：你现在就要换新车吗？

　　　B：不，等有了一些积蓄以后再换新车。

走　　　　　雨停了
出发　　　　小张来了
养花儿　　　买了房子以后
下棋　　　　有空儿的时候

3. 课堂活动　Classroom activity

Do the following math problems in Chinese with your classmates. One student asks a question and another student gives the answer. For example,

三的五倍是多少？

八十的四分之一是多少？

英语系的学生有800人，汉语系的学生是英语系学生的25%，汉语系的学生有多少人？

4. 会话练习　Conversation practice

会话常用语　IDIOMATIC EXPRESSIONS IN CONVERSATION

您别管 (Never mind.)

绝对不行 (Absolutely not.)

这您就不了解了 (This is something you don't understand.)

您听我说 (Let me explain.)

【责备与质问　Reproaching and questioning】

Many expressions in the following conversations are impolite. Pay close attention to the occasions in which they are used appropriately.

（1）A：是你把这事儿告诉她的吧？

　　　B：是啊。应该让她知道这件事儿。

　　　A：她现在身体很不好，为什么你就不能等她好点儿再告诉她？真不知道你是怎么想的。

　　　B：我觉得告诉她这件事儿跟她的身体没关系。

　　　A：怎么没关系？她现在都睡不好觉、吃不好饭了。

（2）A：真不知道你是怎么工作的，你怎么能把这么重要的东西搞丢了？

　　　B：经理，我是很注意的，每天下班的时候我都认真地检查一遍。

　　　A：可是东西不是丢了吗？这叫"认真"啊？

　　　B：真对不起。我想还有办法，比如说……

　　　A：这就是你想的好办法？我看，你是在说梦话。

【拒绝　Refusing】

　　　A：昨天的事儿我想再跟您研究一下。

　　　B：那件事儿我不管。

　　　A：我想您可以再找他谈一次。

　　　B：找他谈？我做不到。就是他找我，我也不想说。我告诉你，不行！绝对不行！

【解释　Making an explanation】

　　　A：老张昨天为什么没有跟大家一起去参观？你们忘了告诉他了？

　　　B：您听我说。情况是这样的，我们打电话通知他的时候，他不在。

　　　A：他应该每天都在啊！

　　　B：这您就不了解了。上月五号他已经退休了。

　　　A：以后这样的活动还应该通知他。

　　　B：我跟您这么说吧，以后这样的活动可以不通知他；通知了他，他也可以不参加。

5. 看图说话　Describe the following pictures

❶ 想要什么就……

❷ 想看什么就……

❸ 想做什么就……

❹ 不想得到什么就……

6. 交际练习　Communication exercises

（1）Discuss with your classmates whether we should agree with Wang Xiaoyun or her mother's idea of consumption.

（2）Tell your classmates whether there is a generation gap between you and your parents (or the older generation) on certain issues.

After you speak, write down what you have said.

阅读与复述 Reading Comprehension and Paraphrasing

🎧36 高薪（gāoxīn）穷人（qióngrén）族

生活里常常看到这样的事儿：越是拿高薪的人，越感到钱不够用，要经常借钱花。他们每月挣得不少，可是花得更多。有钱的时候，他们就乱（luàn）花，想去哪儿玩儿就去哪儿玩儿，什么东西贵就买什么。等钱花完了，他们可能就连饭也吃不上了，日子过得很困难。拿着高薪，有时过着一分钱也没有的生活，这就是年轻的"高薪穷人族"的消费（xiāofèi）方式。

这些人大部分都没有结婚。他们追求（zhuīqiú）个人享受，自己挣钱自己花，不用管别人。对他们来说，花钱是一种快乐。他们觉得自己是在享受一种消费文化，是一种新的消费观念。

高薪穷人族大部分（dà bùfen）既没有银行存款（cúnkuǎn），又没有自己的住房，二十几岁还跟父母住在一起，每月只向父母交很少的一点儿饭钱，大部分收入都花在个人消费上，比如买衣服、下饭馆、搞交际（jiāojì）、上酒吧、看演出、去旅游。这些高薪穷人自己并不觉得这有什么问题。他们的想法是：不管那么多，先享受了生活再说。

他们的父母也常跟他们说，不能"今朝有酒今朝醉"（jīn zhāo yǒu jiǔ jīn zhāo zuì）地过日子，就是21世纪，生活也得艰苦朴素，也得勤俭过日子；艰苦奋斗（fèndòu）是中华民族的美德（měidé），什么时候也不能忘。可是他们认为老人的消费观念跟不上时代，得变一变。他们觉得花明天的钱，实现今天的梦，这对国家、对个人都有好处。他们这种生活方式是一种新的消费观念吗？

三、语法　Grammar

1　疑问代词表示任指（1）

Interrogative pronouns indicating arbitrary reference (1)

The same interrogative pronoun can be used twice in a sentence to refer to the same person, thing, time, place or manner. On its first occurrence, the interrogative pronoun is indefinite; however, on its second occurrence, it refers definitely to the meaning of the first interrogative pronoun. The two phrases or clauses are often connected by "就". For example,

　　你什么时候挣够了钱，什么时候再买车。

　　你想怎么过就怎么过！

　　银行的钱不是谁想借谁就能借到的。

　　我想去哪儿就去哪儿！

　　你爱怎么着就怎么着。

The same interrogative pronoun can have different grammatical functions in the two clauses. For example,

　　谁有知识，我们就向谁学习。

　　哪种办法好，我们就用哪种。

Note:

If there is a subject in the second clause, "就" is usually placed after it. The following sentences are incorrect: "银行的钱不是谁想借就谁能借到的。" "谁有知识，就我们向谁学习。" "哪种办法好，就我们用哪种。"

2　分数、百分数、倍数　Fractions, percentages and multiples

In a fraction, "/" is read as "分之". The denominator is read first, and then the numerator. For example,

　　3/4——四分之三

　　6/25——二十五分之六

　　1/3——三分之一

The percentage sign "%" is read as "百分之". For example,

6%——百分之六

93%——百分之九十三

To read a multiple, the numeral is read first, and then the character "倍". For example,

开车最少比骑自行车快一倍。

8是4的两倍。

今年的学生是去年的三倍，去年有50个学生，今年有多少个学生？

3　一……也/都＋没/不……　The construction "一……也/都＋没/不……"

This construction is frequently used to emphasize complete negation. The character "一" is followed by a measure word and a noun. The noun usually indicates the recipient of the action; sometimes it also acts as the doer of the action. When "一" is used for emphasis, the sentence is spoken in an exaggerative tone. For example,

他一点儿信用都没有。

我这辈子一次债都没有借过。

植物园里一个人也没有。

这次活动我们系一个人也没有参加。

In the sentences with a subject-predicate phrase as predicate, the construction "一……也/都＋没/不……" is often used to emphasize complete negation. For example,

您的钱我一分也不要。

这事儿他好像一点儿也不知道。

4　就是……，也……　The construction "就是……，也……"

In this construction, "就是" indicates a hypothetic condition or concession, and "也" is used to emphasize that the result is not affected by what is mentioned above. For example,

就是21世纪，生活也得艰苦朴素。

就是没钱买米，我也不借债。

明天就是下大雨，我也要去参观展览。

四、字与词　Chinese Characters and Words

构词法（9）：附加式 ③

Word formation method (9): Affixed compound words ③

In Chinese, a suffix-like character is attached to an independent or compound word to form a new word. For example,

（1）生：医生　学生　小学生　中学生　大学生　留学生　研究生

（2）员：队员　演员　售货员　售票员　服务员　技术员　教员　学员

（3）家：画家　美术家　书法家　科学家　文学家　旅行家　教育家

（4）馆：饭馆　茶馆　咖啡馆　图书馆　美术馆　博物馆　展览馆
　　　　熊猫馆

（5）院：医院　学院　戏院　医学院　商学院　文学院　科学院　电影院

Consumption of Chinese People

Since the reform and opening up in the mainland of China more than 30 years ago, Chinese people have experienced a great leap in their living standards. Despite of that, the majority of Chinese people still hold a rather conservative attitude towards consumption, an attitude that has its roots in traditional Chinese culture and values.

To live a secure and happy life, ordinary Chinese would like to get a dwelling of their own in the first place. Therefore, buying an apartment has become the first and most important thing for young people after they start to work. However, as the population in big cities keeps incresing, the housing price is getting higher and higher. Most people still cannot afford an apartment until they have saved quite a sum of money.

Other than housing, education is another aspect in which Chinese people, especially Chinese parents, spend a fortune. The family planning policy has made people more concerned with the education of their only child. They spare no expense when it comes to education. This is one of the reasons why they are unwilling to spend more money in other aspects.

A survey shows that for most Chinese people, overdraft consumption is not an option. About 30% of Chinese people overdraw now and then, and only 5% overdraw frequently. Those who are used to overdraft consumption are mostly young people, who have received a higher education and been highly influenced by the consumption culture in Western countries. They are after fashionable lifestyles and relatively high living standards and meanwhile have a promising expectation for good income in the future. Therefore, young people account for a large proportion of the consumers of luxuries, entertainment and tourism.

The majority of Chinese people hold a more rational consumption concept. They advocate measured and planned consumption, and a small amout of surplus would be preferable. Due to the tradition of frugality and the to-be-improved social security system in China, Chinese people tend to save their money for future use in housing, education, health care and life in old age.

第三十六课

Lesson 36

北京热起来了

It's getting hot in Beijing.

Climate is important for tourism. China is such a big country that the characteristics of the climate in different regions vary significantly. Xiao Yanzi, the tour guide, says that there are good itineraries for tourists all year round. Let's see how she explains this.

一、课文　Text

🎧 37 （一）

马大为：小燕子，我有个朋友要来中国旅游，他问我，什么季节来比较好。中国这么大，气候一定很复杂吧？

小燕子：没错儿。从热带到寒带，各种气候中国差不多都有。①

马大为：北京的气候有什么特点？

> 谈气候
> **Talking about the climate**

小燕子：一年有春、夏、秋、冬四个季节，非常清楚。

马大为：可是我觉得这儿只有冬天，好像没有春天。

小燕子：北京有春天。应该说：这儿的春天很短，冬天很长。

马大为：3月房子里的暖气还没停，现在都4月了，气温才11度，我还穿着羽绒服呢。

小燕子：是啊！从11月到第二年4月，北京天气都很冷，常常刮大风，有时候还下雪。三四月南方各种花儿都开了，可是北京还比较冷，有时候人们还得穿着冬天的衣服。

马大为：就是。你看，我就穿得这么多，连路也走不动了。

小燕子：可是北京一到5月，天气就热起来了。姑娘们也开始穿裙子过夏天了。

马大为：我很喜欢北京的夏天。当然，最好秋天来北京旅游。②

提建议
Making a suggestion

小燕子：对，秋天是北京最好的季节。天气很凉快，不刮风，不下雨，不冷也不热，非常舒服。你朋友秋天来得了吗？

马大为：我想他来得了，不过还得问问他。

小燕子：除了秋天以外，别的季节也可以来中国旅游。因为各个地方的特点不同，一年四季都有很好的旅游路线。比如，春天可以欣赏江南山水，秋天可以游览内蒙草原，夏天去东北，冬天到海南岛。我这儿有一些旅游介绍，你可以寄给他。

马大为：太好了！我一回去就给他打电话，让他秋天来。就是秋天来不了，也没关系，还可以有很多别的选择。

小燕子：对，什么时候能来就什么时候来，想去哪儿就去哪儿。

生词 New Words

1.	季节	jìjié	N	season　一年有四个季节，最好的季节，别的季节
	季	jì	N	season　一年四季，春季，夏季，秋季，冬季
2.	气候	qìhòu	N	climate　中国的气候，北京的气候，气候条件
3.	复杂	fùzá	A	complicated　复杂的气候，复杂的情况，复杂的问题，复杂的动作，复杂的办法
4.	热带	rèdài	N	torrid zone, tropics　热带气候，热带水果，热带植物
5.	寒带	hándài	N	frigid zone　寒带气候，从热带到寒带
6.	各	gè	Pr	each, every　各种气候，各种花儿，各个地方，各位老师
7.	暖气	nuǎnqì	N	heating　有暖气，开暖气，关暖气，暖气停了
8.	羽绒服	yǔróngfú	N	down coat　穿着羽绒服，名牌羽绒服，一件羽绒服
9.	有时候	yǒushíhou	Adv	sometimes　有时候下雪，有时候很冷
	有时	yǒushí	Adv	sometimes　有时下雪，有时很冷
10.	动	dòng	V	to move　走不动，搬不动，拿得动，跑得动
11.	裙子	qúnzi	N	skirt　穿裙子，一条裙子
12.	最好	zuìhǎo	Adv	had better　最好秋天来，最好今天做完
13.	凉快	liángkuai	A	cool　天气很凉快，这儿很凉快，早上很凉快
14.	了	liǎo	V	(used in conjunction with 得 or 不 after a verb) can　来得了，来不了
15.	除了…… 以外	chúle…… yǐwài		except, besides　除了秋天以外，除了这首诗以外，除了喜欢书法以外
16.	路线	lùxiàn	N	route, itinerary　旅游路线，开车的路线
17.	草原	cǎoyuán	N	grassland　大草原，内蒙草原

18. 选择	xuǎnzé	V/N	to select; choice 选择专业，选择地方，选择时间，选择办法；别的选择，有很多选择
19. 江南	Jiāngnán	PN	south of the Changjiang River
20. 内蒙	Nèiměng	PN	Inner Mongolia
21. 东北	Dōngběi	PN	the Northeast

注释　Notes

① 各种气候中国差不多都有。

"China has all different types of climate."

"各+M+N" indicates all of the individuals within a certain scope, in which a measure word is usually needed. For example, 各种方法，各位老师，各种情况，各种书，各种困难. Other examples include,

他试过各种方法。

各个民族有不同的传说。

各位老师，各位同学，大家好！

② 当然，最好秋天来北京旅游。

"Of course, it's best to come and visit Beijing in autumn."

"最好" indicates the best choice or greatest hope. For example,

最好明天不下雨，也不刮风。

最好你自己去办这件事。

38　（二）

丁力波：小云，你在读什么书呢？

王小云：《唐诗选》③。以前我现代诗看得比较多，现在我也喜欢起古

诗来了，特别是唐诗。

丁力波：唐诗在中国文学史上非常重要，是不是？

王小云：是啊，像李白、杜甫都是中国最伟大的诗人。④

丁力波：他们跟莎士比亚一样有名吧？

王小云：没错儿，他们都是世界有名的诗人。不过，他们比莎士比亚的岁数可大多了。

丁力波：莎士比亚是四百多年以前的人啊。

王小云：李白如果活着，该有一千三百多岁了。

丁力波：比莎士比亚早那么多！中国文学的历史真长。这些古诗我们现在恐怕还读不了。我记得小时候，我妈妈教过我一首李白的诗。

王小云：哪一首诗？你还背得出来吗？

> 表示可能
> **Indicating a possibility**

丁力波：我试试。

床前明月光，

疑是地上霜。

举头望明月，

低头思故乡。

王小云：你唐诗记得很熟啊！

丁力波：谢谢。可是除了这首诗以外，别的诗我都背不出来了。

王小云：你是不是想妈妈了？

丁力波：是，昨天我收到了妈妈的信。信写得很长，一共三页。

王小云：杜甫说过"家书抵万金"。"书"是"信"的意思。家里来的信是很珍贵的。

丁力波："家书抵万金"，说得多么好啊！我要给妈妈回一封长信，我有好多话想对她说。

王小云：恐怕五页也写不下吧？

生词 New Words

1. 现代	xiàndài	N	modern 现代诗，现代文学，现代舞蹈，现代音乐，现代艺术
2. 伟大	wěidà	A	great 伟大的科学家，伟大的文学家，伟大的作品，伟大的时代
3. 诗人	shīrén	N	poet 最伟大的诗人，现代诗人
4. 小时候	xiǎoshíhou	N	in one's childhood 小时候妈妈教过我，小时候他很艰苦，小时候的事儿
5. 背	bèi	V	to recite, to learn by heart 背诗，背课文，背一遍，背不下来
6. 床前明月光	Chuáng qián míng yuè guāng		In front of the bed, the bright moonlight shines.
7. 疑是地上霜	Yí shì dì shàng shuāng		(I) wonder if (it) is frost on the ground.
8. 举头望明月	Jǔ tóu wàng míng yuè		(I) raise (my) head and gaze at the bright moon.
9. 低头思故乡	Dī tóu sī gùxiāng		(I) lower my head and think of (my) beloved hometown.

10.	熟	shú	A	familiar　我们很熟，跟他不熟，记得很熟
11.	页	yè	M	page　这本书有280页，第一页
12.	家书抵万金	Jiāshū dǐ wàn jīn		A letter from home is worthy of ten thousand pieces of gold.
13.	珍贵	zhēnguì	A	valuable, precious　珍贵的信，珍贵的纪念品，珍贵的礼物
14.	封	fēng	M	*a measure word for letters*　两封信，一封长信
15.	《唐诗选》	Tángshī Xuǎn	PN	*Selected Tang Poems*
16.	杜甫	Dù Fǔ	PN	Du Fu (a great poet of the Tang Dynasty)
17.	莎士比亚	Shāshìbǐyà	PN	William Shakespeare

补充生词 Supplementary Words

1.	僧敲月下门	Sēng qiāo yuè xià mén		A monk knocks on a gate under the moon (moonlight).
	敲	qiāo	V	to knock
2.	贾岛	Jiǎ Dǎo	PN	Jia Dao (a Chinese poet of the Tang Dynasty)
3.	毛驴	máolǘ	N	donkey
4.	鸟宿池边树	Niǎo sù chí biān shù		A bird perches on a tree at night by the side of the pool.
	鸟	niǎo	N	bird
5.	描写	miáoxiě	V	to describe
6.	推	tuī	V	to push
7.	韩愈	Hán Yù	PN	Han Yu (a Chinese litterateur of the Tang Dynasty)

8. 轿子	jiàozi	N	sedan chair
9. 经过	jīngguò	V	to pass, to go by
10. 官	guān	N	government official
11. 拉	lā	V	to pull
12. 思考	sīkǎo	V	to think deeply

注释　Notes

③ 《唐诗选》

Selected Tang Poems

"唐诗" is the poetry of the Tang Dynasty. Chinese poetry reached its prime in the history of Chinese literature during the Tang Dynasty (618–907), and many great poets appeared in this period, such as Li Bai and Du Fu. Approximately 50,000 Tang poems by more than 2,200 outstanding poets have been handed down.

④ 像李白、杜甫都是中国最伟大的诗人。

"Li Bai and Du Fu were among the greatest Chinese poets."

The verb "像" can be used to cite examples, but it is different from "比如" and generally cannot be put at the end of a sentence. For example,

像丁力波、马大为，他们都是语言学院的学生。

中国的大城市很多，像北京、上海、广州都是。

二、练习 Exercises

练习与运用 **Drills and Practice** 🎧 39

核心句 KEY SENTENCES

1. 从热带到寒带，各种气候中国差不多都有。
2. 你看，我就穿得这么多，连路也走不动了。
3. 北京一到5月，天气就热起来了。
4. 最好秋天来北京旅游。
5. 你朋友秋天来得了吗？
6. 除了秋天以外，别的季节也可以来中国旅游。
7. 我一回去就给他打电话。
8. 像李白、杜甫都是中国最伟大的诗人。
9. 除了这首诗以外，别的诗我都背不出来了。
10. 恐怕五页也写不下吧？

1. 熟读下列词组 Read the following phrases until you learn them by heart

（1）坐不下六个人　　放不下三张桌子　　住不下这么多人
　　　站得下一万人　　停得下十五辆车

（2）吃不了这么多水果　赢不了他们队　　上不了班
　　　喝得了这瓶可乐　　办得了这件事儿

（3）搬不动这个书架　　走不动这么远的路　拿不动一百斤米
　　　开得动这辆汽车　　骑得动自行车

（4）热起来了　　　冷起来了　　好起来了　　高兴起来了
　　　喜欢起古诗来了　唱起歌来了　下起雨来了　刮起风来了

（5）各位同学　　各个地方　　各个学校　　各个城市

　　　各种气候　　各种书　　各种情况

2. 句型替换　Pattern drills

（1）A：一页 写得下 这么多话吗？

　　　B：恐怕写不下。

一辆车	坐	五个人
一个书架	放	这么多书
这张纸	包	这件礼物
这个电梯	站	15个人

（2）A：你朋友 秋天 来得了来不了北京？

　　　B：我想他 来得了。

大学生队	明天	赢	他们
陈老师	星期六	去	长城
他	下午	办	这事儿
小张	一个月	花	这些钱

（3）A：你怎么连路也走不动了？

　　　B：我穿得太多了。

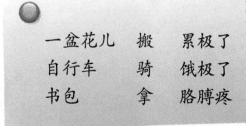

一盆花儿	搬	累极了
自行车	骑	饿极了
书包	拿	胳膊疼

（4）A：你打算什么时候给他寄旅游介绍?

　　　B：他一打来电话，我就给他寄旅游
　　　　 介绍。

回国	学校	放假
买汽车	银行	贷款
出国留学	这儿学习	结业

（5）A：北京夏天的气候怎么样?

　　　B：北京一到5月就热起来了。

冬天	11月	冷
秋天	9月	凉
春天	3月	刮（风）
夏天	6月	下（雨）

（6）A：你们都去内蒙草原旅游过吗?

　　　B：除了小张以外，我们都去旅游过。

习惯吃中餐	新来的同学	习惯了
交了罚款	马大为	还没有交
每天看电视	星期五和星期六	不看
会中国武术	丁力波	不会

（7）A：除了李白的这首诗以外，你还能背什么?

　　　B：我还能背杜甫的一首诗。

唐诗	喜欢什么	喜欢	现代诗
游泳	爱好什么	爱好	健美操
江南	去过哪儿	去过	东北
旗袍	常穿什么	常穿	短裙

3. 课堂活动　Classroom activities

（1）One student makes a suggestion, then another student uses "最好" to add further details to the suggestion. For example,

  A：我们应该搞一次聚会。

  B：最好是星期五的晚上。

  C：最好把老师也请来。

  ……　　……

（2）"一……就……" is used to indicate that two events happen in close succession. For example,

  A：天气一冷，

  B：外边人就少了。

  C：他就感冒了。

  ……　　……

4. 会话练习　Conversation practice

> **会话常用语 IDIOMATIC EXPRESSIONS IN CONVERSATION**
>
> 没错儿 (Exactly.)
>
> 应该说 (the fact is...)
>
> 就是 (You bet.)

【谈气候　Talking about the climate】

  A：可能是因为环境污染，现在气候变得越来越奇怪了。

  B：是啊。咱们这儿是北方，可是今天的气温最高到了35度，比南方
    还高，成了全国最热的地方了。

  A：而且一下起雨来就停不住，也跟南方差不多了。

  B：冬天的气温也越来越高，很少下雪。

A：我觉得现在的气候是有点儿不正常。

【提建议　Making a suggestion】

A：这几天我正在选课呢。你说选哪些课好？

B：除了听力课以外，口语课也是一定要选的。咱们的口语水平还要
继续提高。

A：我也是这样想的。语法课呢？

B：如果你有时间，最好也选语法课。对了，我还建议你选汉字课。

【表示可能　Indicating a possibility】

A：喂，是小钱吗？我是小王，明天的聚会我参加不了了。

B：你怎么了？

A：我感冒了，恐怕明天去不了了。

B：是吗？没关系，你好好儿休息吧。

A：谢谢你。对了，吃饭的时候你见得到力波吗？

B：有什么事儿？

A：我想请他帮个忙，星期四跟我一起到邮局去把我的书取回来。我
一个人拿不动。

B：好的，我一定告诉他。

5. 看图说话　Describe the following pictures

❶ 踢……了

❷ 睡……着

❸ 跑……动

6. 交际练习　Communication exercises

(1) Describe the climate of your mother country or the city you live in.

(2) Describe a summer resort in your mother country.

After you speak, write down what you have said.

阅读与复述 Reading Comprehension and Paraphrasing

40　僧敲月下门（Sēng Qiāo Yuè Xià Mén）

贾岛（Jiǎ Dǎo）是中国唐代有名的诗人。传说，他常骑在毛驴（máolú）上做诗。有一天，他骑着毛驴，想写一首描写月夜景色的诗。他已经想出了两句：

鸟宿池边树，　（Niǎo sù chí biān shù）
僧敲月下门。

这是两句好诗，很好地描写（miáoxiě）出一幅月夜的景色：水池边有一棵大树，月光照在树上，树上的小鸟已经安静地睡觉了；有一个和尚来到寺庙门前，用手轻轻地敲寺庙的大门。贾岛一边念着这两句诗，一边往前走，心里非常高兴。但是他又觉得，夜里这么安静，这个和尚不应该"敲"门，用手"推（tuī）"门比较好。他又念了几遍，还是觉得"敲"比"推"好。

他骑在小毛驴上，也不看路，只想着用手"推门"还是用手"敲门"。他的毛驴已经从山下的小路走上了大路。这时候，韩愈（Hán Yù）坐着轿子（jiàozi）正从这儿经过（jīngguò）。贾岛的毛驴跟韩愈的轿子撞上了。韩愈可是大官（guān），保护他的人马上走过来，把贾岛从毛驴上拉（lā）了下来，问他想要干什么。

贾岛还不知道出了什么事，就被带到轿子前边。他看见轿子里坐着一位大官，就说："真对不起，刚才我正在想自己诗中的一个字呢，没看见您，跟您撞上了……"

韩愈也是一位诗人，对作诗很感兴趣。一听说是写诗，他就走下轿子，笑着问贾岛："什么诗呀？你念给我听听。"贾岛就把自己的诗句念给韩愈听。他还问韩愈，是"僧敲月下门"好呢，还是"僧推月下门"好呢？

韩愈连想也没想，就说："'敲'比'推'好。你想，在没有人也没有声音的月夜，有几下敲门的声音，不是更让人觉得安静吗？"

后来"推敲"就成了一个新词，表示"研究、思考（sīkǎo）"的意思，贾岛和韩愈也成了很好的朋友。

三、语法　Grammar

1　可能补语（2）Complement of possibility (2)

Verbs like "下", "了" and "动" can be used as complements of possibility.

"V+得/不+下" indicates whether a certain quantity or amount of things can be put in

some place. The verbs frequently used in this construction are: 站，坐，睡，停，放，住.
For example,

书包里放不下这么多东西。

这儿停不下十辆汽车。

宿舍住得下这么多人吗？

"V+得/不+了" indicates whether somebody can do something. (In general, the verb "了"
can only be used as a complement of possibility.) For example,

你朋友秋天来得了吗？

她的腿被撞伤了，她现在走不了路。

老师病了，明天上不了课了。

Sometimes the verb "了" means "完". For example,

这么一大杯葡萄酒，她喝不了。

学院离这儿不远，用不了半个小时就到了。

"V+得/不+动" shows whether or not a movement or an action will cause somebody or
something to change its original position. For example,

你看我就穿得这么多，连路都走不动了。

他一个人搬不动这张大桌子。

你不用帮我了，我自己拿得动这些东西。

Note:
The optative verbs "能" and "可以" indicate possibilities. However, when indicating somebody
cannot do something because the objective conditions are unavailable, complements of possibility
instead of optative verbs are generally used. For example,

小孩儿搬不动这个大花盆。（One cannot say: "小孩儿不能搬这个大花盆。"）

这儿声音太大，我听不见。（One cannot say: "这儿声音太大，我不能听见。"）

Either complements of possibility or optative verbs can be used to indicate whether somebody can
or cannot do something due to his ability or condition. For example,

我学过英语，我能翻译。(我学过英语，我翻译得了。)

今天天气很好，我们能去长城。(今天天气很好，我们去得了长城。)

你不用帮助我，我自己能搬。(你不用帮助我，我自己搬得动。)

When requesting someone to do a movement or an action, or when dissuading someone from doing a movement or an action, one can only use an optative verb. The complement of possibility cannot be used. For example,

　　外边刮风了，你不能出去。（You cannot say：“外边刮风了，你出不去。”）

　　我可以进来吗？（You cannot say：“我进得来吗？”）

2 "起来" 的引申用法　Extended usage of "起来"

"V/A+起来" indicates the beginning and continuation of a movement, an action or a state. For example,

　　刚到五月，天气就热起来了。

　　快要考试了，他现在忙起来了。

　　以前我喜欢现代诗，现在我也喜欢起古诗来了。

　　切蛋糕的时候，大家都唱起生日歌来了。

3 一……就……　The construction "一……就……"

"一……就……"（"as soon as"）indicates that two movements or actions occur in close succession. The movements or actions can be performed by the same subject or two different subjects. For example,

　　陈老师一进教室就开始上课。(the same subject)

　　我一着急，就回答错了。(the same subject)

　　北京一到五月，天气就热起来了。(two different subjects)

　　她一叫，我们就都出来了。(two different subjects)

4 "除了……以外，还/都/也……"
The construction "除了……以外，还/都/也……"

"除了……以外，还/都/也……" indicates in addition to what has been mentioned, what follows is also included. "以外" may be omitted. For example,

　　除了秋天以外，别的季节也可以来中国旅游。

除了喜欢画画儿以外，他还特别喜欢中国书法。

除了现代的新诗，她也爱读唐诗。

"除了……以外，都……" indicates exclusion of something mentioned first and emphasizes the homogeneity of what follows. For example,

除了这首诗以外，别的诗我都背不出来了。

除了星期六和星期日以外，我们每天上午都有汉语课。

除了不喜欢吃羊肉，她什么肉都爱吃。

四、字与词　Chinese Characters and Words

构词法（10）：缩减式
Word formation method (10): Abbreviated words

（1）Omission：清华——清华大学

（2）Abbreviation：北大——北京大学，北语——北京语言大学

（3）Simplified alternatives：　京——北京市，沪——上海市，粤——广东省，

中美——中国和美国，中英——中国和英国

学唱中文歌
Sing a Song

在那遥远的地方

Zài nà yáoyuǎn de dìfang

A Place Far Far Away

Andarntio

哈萨克族民歌
王洛宾 改编

1=E

6 1 2 1 6 6 1 2· 1 6 6 1 1 7 6 ——

在 那　遥 远 的 地　方，　　有 位 好 姑 娘，

她 那　粉 红 的 笑　脸，　　好 像 红 太 阳，

我 愿　抛 弃 了 财　产，　　跟 她 去 放 羊，

我 愿　做 一 只 小　羊，　　跟 在 她 身 旁，

6 1 2 1 6 5 6 5 4 5　6 1 4 5 6 5 4 3　2 —— —

人 们 走 过 她 的 帐 房　都 要 回 头 留 恋 地 张　望。

她 那 活 泼 动 人 的 眼 睛　好 像 晚 上 明 媚 的 月　亮。

每 天 看 着 那 粉 红 的 笑 脸　和 那 美 丽 金 边 的 衣　裳。

我 愿 她 拿 着 细 细 的 皮 鞭　不 断 轻 轻 打 在 我 身　上。

Climate of China

Most parts of China are located in the north temperate zone, where the mild climate and distinct seasons create a pleasant environment for people to live in.

The climate of China is complicated and varies. Due to its vast territory and considerable large span of latitude, China consists of six climate zones, which are respectively, from the south to the north, the equatorial zone, the tropical zone, the subtropical zone, the warm temperate zone, the temperate zone and the cold temperate zone. Since the distances to the sea, the elevations, the terrain patterns and the directions of mountains vary from one area to another, different climate types have taken shape, including the monsoon climate in the east, the temperate continental climate in the northwest and the frigid climate on Qinghai−Tibet Plateau, etc. Besides, humidity also creates a clear distinction among different areas.

China is located in the eastern part of Eurasia. The Pacific Ocean lies to its east and the Indian Ocean not far away to its southwest. Because of the remarkable influences from the continent and the oceans, China has the most typical monsoon climate in the world. In summer, it is hot and rainy; while in winter, it is cold with a little rain. Here, hot weather often comes hand in hand with abundant rain. This kind of climate provides favorable conditions for agriculture, and most crops, animals and plants in the world grow well here. No wonder China abounds with crops and animal and plant resources.

However, China's climate also has its drawback. Frequent occurrences of disastrous weather cause great loss in production and people's life. Among all kinds of disastrous weather, droughts, floods, typhoons and cold waves and the resultant gales, sandstorms and frost are the major ones that China suffers from.

第三十七课
Lesson 37

谁来买单

Who will pay the bill?

This weekend, Lin Na wants to invite some Chinese friends to dinner at a restaurant, but after they eat, everyone fights to pay the bill. What is going on?

一、课文　Text

🎧 41 （一）

林　娜：小云、力波、宋华，你们今天晚上都有空儿吗？咱们到外边
　　　　吃晚饭去。①

王小云：好啊，我们都去，人越多越热闹。去哪家饭馆呢？

宋　华：去哪家都行。

丁力波：对，只要不是学校餐厅的菜，我什么都想吃。咱们走吧。

　　＊　　　　　＊　　　　　＊　　　　　＊　　　　　＊　　　　　＊

林　娜：大为，你再来一点儿。

马大为：今天的菜味道好极了，我吃得太多，实在吃不下了。

林　娜：大家都吃好了吧？服务员，买单。②

服务员：好，这是账单。

宋　华：把账单给我。

> 在饭馆
> **At a restaurant**

王小云：我来付。

服务员：谢谢。您这是二百，请稍等。

林　娜：怎么回事儿？③ 我请你们吃晚饭，你们怎么都抢着买单？你

们还比我动作快！

王小云：谁买单都一样。

林　娜：今天是我约大家来的，就该由我付钱。④

王小云：你就下回再付吧。

丁力波：我怎么也不明白，为什么你们人人都要买单？好吧，咱们就

AA制吧。⑤

王小云：不行，这次我来，下次再AA制。

林　娜：为什么？小云，我请客，你买单，

这不成了笑话了吗？

宋　华：你要听笑话，我可以给你们讲一个。有人说，要是看见很多

人在球场上抢一个橄榄球，那可能是美国人；要是看见很多

人在饭馆里抢一张纸，那就很可能是中国人。

丁力波：为什么中国人喜欢这样做呢？

宋　华：我们跟朋友在一起的时候，一般不希望给别人添麻烦，都愿

意自己多拿出一些。当然有的人也可能是想表示自己大方。

所以，如果几个中国人一起在饭馆吃饭，事先没有说清楚由

谁请客，最后大家就会抢着买单。你们看，对面的那几位抢

得比我们还热闹呢。

> 表示奇怪
> **Expressing a surprise**

生词 New Words

1. 买单	mǎidān	V	(*coll.*) to pay a bill 我来买单，谁来买单
2. 晚饭	wǎnfàn	N	supper, dinner 吃晚饭，一顿（dùn）晚饭
3. 越……越……	yuè……yuè……		the more ... the more ... 越多越热闹，越唱越高兴，越学越好，越活越年轻
4. 味道	wèidao	N	taste, flavor 味道很好，味道好极了，菜的味道
5. 账单	zhàngdān	N	bill 饭馆的账单，医院的账单
账	zhàng	N	account, bill 付账
单	dān	N	list 通知单，成绩单
6. 回	huí	M	*a measure word used for happenings or events* 一回事，两回事，怎么一回事，去过一回，吃过一回，用过一回
7. 抢	qiǎng	V	to snatch, to make efforts to be the first, to fight for 抢东西，抢钱，抢着买单，抢着付账，抢着回答
8. 约	yuē	V	to ask or invite (in advance) 约大家来，约他聊天儿，约朋友聚会，约同学看电影，约我散步
9. 由	yóu	Prep	(to be done) by (sb.) 由我付，由他来做，由学校管理，由公司解决
10. 明白	míngbai	V/A	to understand; clear, explicit 怎么也不明白，明白这件事；他讲得很明白
11. AA制	AA zhì	N	to go Dutch
12. 请客	qǐngkè	VO	to invite sb. to dinner, usually with the intention to pay 我请客
13. 笑话	xiàohua	N/V	joke; to make fun of (sb.) 说笑话，讲笑话，一个笑话，成了笑话；笑话别人

14.	球场	qiúchǎng	N	ground or court for ball games 球场上
15.	橄榄球	gǎnlǎnqiú	N	rugby, American football 踢橄榄球，橄榄球赛
	橄榄	gǎnlǎn	N	olive
16.	添	tiān	V	to add, to increase 添麻烦，添衣服，添一点儿饭，添一台电脑
17.	大方	dàfang	A	generous 大方的人，动作大方
18.	事先	shìxiān	N	in advance, beforehand 事先知道，事先告诉，事先没有说清楚
19.	最后	zuìhòu	N	final, last 最后一课，最后一次，排在最后

注释 Notes

① 咱们到外边吃晚饭去。

"Let's go out for dinner."

"外边" refers to a dining hall or restaurant outside of the school.

② 服务员，买单。

"Bill, please."

"买单" usually refers to paying the bill after eating at a restaurant. The expression is originated from the Cantonese dialect, but has become popular in the colloquial northern dialect.

③ 怎么回事儿？

"What's going on?"

This is an expression indicating the speaker's surprise or puzzle.

④ 今天是我约大家来的，就该由我付钱。

"I asked you out today, so I'll take care of the bill."

"由+NP+V" indicates that it's somebody or some organization's responsibility to do something. For example,

电影票由宋华去买。

这个问题应该由学校解决。

⑤ 咱们就AA制吧。

"Let's go Dutch."

"AA制" (pronounced AA zhì) means people share expenses equally or each pays his/her own expenses after dinner. In modern Chinese, there are quite a few expressions beginning with the Western letters, such as "PC机 (peronal computer)" and "IP电话 (Voice over Internet Protocol)". Some are the abbreviations of the Western language, such as CD, DVD and WTO. These are pronounced following the rules of pronouncing the Western language.

 42 （二）

宋　华：你们喜欢吃羊肉吗？

马大为：喜欢。上星期六，我们班同学跟陈老师一起去内蒙草原旅游，还吃了烤全羊呢！

宋　华：烤全羊？你们几个人吃得了吗？

马大为：吃得了。我们班的同学除了林娜以外都去了。包括陈老师，一共16个人呢。

丁力波：我们是按蒙族的习惯吃的。⑥大家一坐好，两个蒙族姑娘就
　　　　抬出了烤好的羊。还有两个姑娘，一个举着酒杯，一个拿着
　　　　酒壶，慢慢地向我们走过来。她们站在我们的桌子前边，唱
　　　　起蒙族民歌来。

宋　华：有意思，说下去。

丁力波：这时候，饭店的经理向大家表示欢迎。他说："欢迎各国朋
　　　　友来我们内蒙草原旅游。今天晚上，请大家按蒙族的习惯吃
　　　　烤全羊。首先，由我们这四位姑娘向你们敬酒，请你们中间
　　　　岁数最大、最受尊敬的人喝第一杯酒，吃第一块烤羊肉。"

宋　华：谁喝了第一杯酒？

马大为：当然是陈老师，她比我们岁数大。

丁力波：四位姑娘唱着蒙族民歌，向陈老师敬
　　　　酒。然后，请陈老师吃第一块羊肉。

动作的顺序
Sequence of actions

马大为：陈老师吃了羊肉以后，四位姑娘又接着唱下去，⑦给我们每
　　　　个人敬酒、敬烤羊肉。我们也跟着唱起来。大家越唱越高
　　　　兴，这个晚上过得非常愉快。

宋　华：你们吃过内蒙的烤全羊了，下个星期六，我请大家吃地道的
　　　　新疆烤羊肉。

生词 New Words

1.	羊肉	yángròu	N	mutton　烤羊肉
2.	班	bān	N	class　我们班，一个班
3.	烤全羊	kǎoquányáng	N	roasted whole lamb
4.	按	àn	Prep	according to　按这儿的习惯，按我们的风俗，按老师的意见
5.	抬	tái	V	to carry　抬起头来，抬桌子，抬床
6.	举	jǔ	V	to hold up, to raise　举杯子，举手，举重
7.	酒杯	jiǔbēi	N	wine glass/cup　举起酒杯，一个酒杯
8.	民歌	míngē	N	folk song　西藏民歌，内蒙民歌，台湾民歌，东北民歌，俄罗斯民歌
9.	饭店	fàndiàn	N	hotel　北京饭店，长城饭店
10.	首先	shǒuxiān	Conj	first of all, firstly
11.	敬酒	jìng jiǔ	V O	to propose a toast　向大家敬酒
	敬	jìng	V	to offer politely　敬茶，敬酒，敬烟
*12.	受	shòu	V	to receive, to be subjected to　受教育，受称赞，受污染
13.	尊敬	zūnjìng	V	to respect, to honor　尊敬老师，尊敬老人，受尊敬的人
14.	然后	ránhòu	Conj	then, after that
15.	接着	jiēzhe	V	to follow, to carry on　接着唱，接着说，接着商量，接着敬酒
16.	愉快	yúkuài	A	happy, pleasant　过得很愉快，生活愉快，愉快的事儿
17.	蒙族	Měngzú	PN	Mongolian ethnic group
18.	新疆	Xīnjiāng	PN	Xinjiang (an autonomous region of China)

补充生词 Supplementary Words

1. 点	diǎn	V	to order
2. 竹子	zhúzi	N	bamboo
3. 巧云	Qiǎoyún	PN	Qiaoyun (name of a young maid)
4. 保姆	bǎomǔ	N	maid
5. 主人	zhǔrén	N	host, master
6. 肉丝炒竹笋	ròusī chǎo zhúsǔn		stir-fried shredded pork with bamboo shoots
肉丝	ròusī	N	shredded pork
炒	chǎo	V	to stir-fry
竹笋	zhúsǔn	N	bamboo shoot
7. 词典	cídiǎn	N	dictionary
8. 计划生育	jìhuà shēngyù		family planning
计划	jìhuà	V	to plan
生育	shēngyù	V	to give birth to
9. 优生优育	yōushēng yōuyù		to bear and rear healthy babies
优	yōu	A	excellent

注释 Notes

⑥ 我们是按蒙族的习惯吃的。

"We ate it following the Mongolian custom."

"按+NP+V" indicates following some standard to do something. For example,

我们按那儿的风俗用手抓饭吃。

我们按医生的话一天吃三次药。

⑦ 四位姑娘又接着唱下去。

"Then the four girls went on singing."

The verb "接着" is used as an adverbial, and "接着+V" indicates either that the latter action closely follows the former one in time, or that the latter action is the continuation of the former one. For example,

你先说，我接着说。

他先介绍北京，接着介绍上海。

今天我们先学到这儿，明天我们接着学。

The sequence of narrating the actions in serial: "首先/先——再/又/接着——然后/接着——最后".

二、练习　Exercises

练习与运用　**Drills and Practice** 43

核心句 KEY SENTENCES

1. 去哪家饭馆都行。
2. 只要不是学校餐厅的菜，我什么都想吃。
3. 谁买单都一样。
4. 今天是我约大家来的，就该由我付钱。
5. 我怎么也不明白，为什么你们人人都要买单？
6. 对面的那几位抢得比我们还热闹呢。
7. 她比我们岁数大。
8. 四位姑娘又接着唱下去。
9. 大家越唱越高兴。

1. 熟读下列词组　Read the following phrases until you learn them by heart

（1）讲下去　看下去　听下去　唱下去　念下去　背下去　聊下去　住下去
比赛下去　　生活下去　　演奏下去　　翻译下去

（2）谁都不认识　什么都吃过　哪儿也没去过　怎么做都可以

（3）由陈老师教　由司机开　由你去做　由学校解决　由公司付账

（4）跑得比他慢　睡得比以前早　做得比他们认真　发展得比农村快

　　　棋下得比我差　球踢得比红队好　花儿开得比去年美　债借得比他们多

（5）按医生的话吃药　　　　　　按老师的意见准备

　　　按蒙族习惯敬酒　　　　　　按这儿的风俗送礼

2. 句型替换　Pattern drills

（1）A：你们喜欢听吗？

　　　B：很有意思，请<u>说下去</u>。

> 讲下去
> 唱下去
> 念下去
> 背下去

（2）A：我们<u>去哪家饭馆</u>呢？

　　　B：<u>哪家饭馆</u>都行。

要什么菜	什么菜
让谁参加	谁参加
去哪儿旅游	去哪儿
要怎么过生日	怎么过

（3）A：<u>对面的那几位</u> <u>抢得</u> <u>热闹</u>不<u>热闹</u>？

　　　B：<u>对面的那几位</u> <u>抢得</u>比<u>我们</u>更<u>热闹</u>。

白队	踢	好	红队
城市的经济	发展	快	农村
女学生	学习	认真	男学生
今年的花儿	开	好看	去年

（4）A：她比<u>你们</u> <u>岁数大</u>吗？
　　　B：她没有<u>我们</u> <u>岁数大</u>。

张小姐	身体好
林娜	嗓子好
她姐姐	学习努力

（5）A：<u>今天的账单</u>由<u>谁</u> <u>付</u>？
　　　B：<u>今天的账单</u>由<u>我</u> <u>付</u>。

这个问题	去回答	丁力波
这辆新车	来开	老司机
学生宿舍	打扫	服务员
这个商店	管理	张经理

（6）A：<u>大家</u> <u>唱</u>得怎么样了？
　　　B：<u>大家</u>越<u>唱</u>越<u>高兴</u>。

雨	下	大
风	刮	大
他们	聊	热闹
他的汉语	说	流利

3. 课堂活动　Classroom activity

Describe an event in order to your classmates using "首先/先……再/又/接着……然后/接着……最后……". For example,

　　A：昨天我们去城里了，

　　B：我们先在书店买了很多书，

　　C：又买了光盘，

　　D：然后去饭馆吃饭，

　　E：接着去商场买东西，

　　F：最后看了一个电影。

　　……　　……

4. 会话练习 Conversation practice

会话常用语 IDIOMATIC EXPRESSIONS IN CONVERSATION

去哪家都行 (Anywhere is fine.)

我什么都想吃 (I want to eat anything.)

怎么回事儿 (What's going on?)

我怎么也不明白 (I just don't understand.)

【在饭馆 At a restaurant】

（1）A：小张，你想吃点儿什么？你来点（diǎn）菜吧。

B：我吃什么都行。小王点吧，你常来这儿，比较熟，你喜欢吃什么我们就吃什么。

C：我可喜欢吃辣的，越辣越好。你们吃得了吗？

B：没有关系，我也是"怕不辣"。

D：我病了不能吃辣的，我就点个烤鸭吧。

（2）A：来，为咱们的友谊，干杯！

B：干杯！

A：这几个菜味道还可以。小张，你再多吃点儿，别客气啊！

B：我已经吃得不少了，实在吃不下了。

（3）A：大家都吃好了吧？小姐，买单。

B：今天我来付账。

A：不是已经说好了吗？这次由我买单。

C：我看这样吧，谁也别抢着付了，咱们今天就AA制。

【表示奇怪 Expressing a surprise】

A：小钱来了吗？

B：他没有来，他说他不参加这次比赛了。

A：怎么回事儿？他昨天不是表示愿意参加的吗？怎么变得这么快？

B：他说他不希望给别人添麻烦。

A：为什么？

B：可能他觉得自己的水平不太高，怕踢不好。

A：我怎么也不明白，他为什么这样想呢？

5. 看图说话　Describe the following picture

6. 交际练习　Communication exercises

Describe the things you usually do or the customs you follow when going out to dinner with your friends.

After you speak, write down what you have said.

阅读与复述 Reading Comprehension and Paraphrasing

🎧44 竹子（zhúzi）的孩子

巧云（Qiǎoyún）在上海打工，她在一个外国人家里当保姆（bǎomǔ）。她会说一点儿英语，可这家主人（zhǔrén）连一句汉语也不会说。一天，巧云做了一个肉丝炒竹笋（ròusī chǎo zhúsǔn），她做得很好吃。主人指着竹笋用英语问巧云："这个很好吃，它是什么？"

巧云不会用英语说"竹笋"这个词，怎么办呢？她心里一着急就对主人说："对不起，先生，我也不知道它是什么。"

"这是你做的菜，是你去商店买的，你怎么会不知道呢？"主人有点儿不高兴地说。

巧云笑着说："我不知道英语怎么说。请等一等，我去查一查词典（cídiǎn）。"

她查完了词典，也只会说"'竹笋'是竹子的孩子"。主人说，吃竹子的孩子不太好，我们应该保护环境、绿化环境，怎么能吃竹子的孩子呢？巧云想告诉主人，竹笋太多是长不出好竹子来的，一定要把那些长得不好的竹笋挖出来。可是，巧云还不能用英语讲清楚这个问题。说汉语，主人又听不懂，她真不知道该怎么办。突然，她想到计划生育（jìhuà shēngyù）中的一句话，就高兴地用英语对主人说："竹子也要计划生育，只有优生优育（yōushēng yōuyù），才能长出好竹子。"主人一听就明白了，并且大笑起来，还称赞巧云，说她讲得比老师还清楚，很有意思。

三、语法 Grammar

1 "下去" 的引申用法 The extended usage of "下去"

The complex directional complement "下去" expresses the continuation of an action. "V/A+下去" indicates that an action which has already started will go on, or that a state which has already come into being will last. For example,

有意思，请说下去。

陈老师吃了羊肉以后，四位姑娘又接着唱下去。

大家只要学下去，就一定能学会。

天气再这样冷下去，我们就该穿羽绒服了。

2 疑问代词表示任指（2）
Interrogative pronouns indicating arbitrary reference (2)

When used in declarative sentences, the interrogative pronouns 谁，什么，哪儿 and 怎么 denote "anyone, anything, anywhere". The adverbs "都" and "也" are commonly used with them. For example,

谁买单都一样。

去哪家饭馆吃饭都行。

他刚来北京，哪儿都想看看。

他什么都不想吃。

这件事真奇怪，我怎么也不明白。

3 用介词"比"表示比较（2）
Making comparison by using the preposition "比" (2)

In addition to the adjectival and verbal phrases, one can also use the subject-predicate phrases to compare the differences between two things with regard to some aspect.

S + Prep "比" + Pr/N + S-PP

Subject	Predicate		
	Prep "比"	Pr/N	S-PP
陈老师	比	我们	岁数　大。
你们	还比	我	动作　快。
这条裙子	比	那条	颜色　好吗？
我外婆	不比	我妈妈	身体　差。

In a sentence with a modal complement to indicate the result of the comparison, "比+Pr/N" is used after the verb and before the modal complement. The meaning of the sentence is basically unchanged. For example,

对面的那几位比我们抢得还热闹呢。（对面的那几位抢得比我们还热闹呢。）

他比他朋友来得早。（他来得比他朋友早。）

张先生翻译唐诗比王先生翻译得好。（张先生翻译唐诗翻译得比王先生好。）

4 越……越……　The construction "越……越……"

This construction indicates that the degree (expressed by the word or words following the second "越") is changing along with the changes of the circumstances (expressed by the word or words following the first "越"). For example,

他很着急，所以越说越快。

雨越下越大了。

大家越唱越高兴。

四、字与词　Chinese Characters and Words

构词法（11）：综合式
Word formation method (11): Composite compound words

A word formed in this method is a compound word, consisting of a noun preceded by its modifiers. Most words of this category are nouns. For example,

照相机　办公室　借书证　通知单　服务员　出租车　展览馆

园艺师　科学家　植物园　中秋节　外交官　橄榄球　太极剑

电影院　兵马俑　羽绒服　建国门　音乐会　图书馆　美术馆

汉语课　火车站　外国人　葡萄酒　君子兰　明信片　人民币

小意思　小学生　小汽车　小时候

商品经济　中华民族　汉语词典　公共汽车　古典音乐

Going Dutch and Standing Treat

Going Dutch is called "AA制" in Chinese and "制" here means "principle" or "rule". The term indicates that people share expenses equally or each pays his/her own expenses after dinner or entertainment.

Going Dutch, a fashion of typical Western style, has its roots in the Western culture. In China, well-educated people are more adapted to this fashion than less-educated people. But generally speaking, it is not well accepted by Chinese people as it goes against the traditional Chinese culture.

In a Chinese restaurant, it is common to see people fighting for the bill. Chinese people attach much importance to "reciprocity". They prefer taking turns treating each other rather than haggling over every penny after a meal. For them, paying the bill is a way to express friendly feelings. On formal business occasions, it is absolutely out of the question for partners to split the bill for their meal or entertainment. Paying the bill is a good way to exhibit the sincerity for cooperation. Chinese people show their friendship by sharing everything they have with each other. Going Dutch makes them feel like drifting away from their friends and therefore is from the essence at odds with the Chinese culture and tradition.

However, young people nowadays in China begin to try going Dutch when they dine together with colleagues, close friends or a bunch of classmates.

第三十八课
Lesson
38

你听，他叫我"太太"

Listen, he called me "Madam".

Yulan is Xiao Yanzi's cousin. Jack is Dawei's friend. After they got to know each other, they fell in love with each other and got married. Something interesting happened when the newly-weds came to the village to visit Yulan's parents: Do you want to know what it was?

一、课文 Text

45 （一）

杰　克：大为、小燕子，告诉你们一个好消息——我结婚了！玉兰嫁

　　　　给我了！

小燕子：等一等，你结婚了？你们是什么时候结婚的？我们怎么都不

　　　　知道？

杰　克：我结婚，我自己知道就行了。再说，我们是旅行结婚，一回

　　　　来就告诉你们，不算晚吧？

小燕子：祝你们新婚愉快，生活幸福。

祝贺新婚
Congratulating the newly-weds

杰　克：谢谢！

小燕子：你只让我们知道还不行，还得……

杰　克：对，我们早就去政府登记了，也拿到了结婚证。

小燕子：我想说的不是这个意思。

杰　克：那是什么意思？

小燕子：我是说，你还得请客。

杰　克：那当然。这是我们的喜糖，来，请吃糖。

小燕子：喜糖我们收下了，但这还不算是请客。

马大为：杰克，按中国人的习惯，结婚要举行婚礼。墙上、门上要贴红双喜字，新娘要坐花轿，还要摆宴席，请很多客人来。婚礼热闹得很。①

杰　克：要举行婚礼，我明白。我们西方人一般是在教堂举行婚礼。说到宴席，我们只请亲戚朋友在一起喝杯酒，②唱唱歌，跳跳舞，高兴高兴。除了特别有钱的人以外，一般都不摆宴席。

小燕子：我表姐的家在农村，结婚宴席可不只是喝杯酒。

杰　克：还有什么？

小燕子：你等着你岳父、岳母教你吧。③

生词 New Words

1.	太太	tàitai	N	Mrs., madam　王太太，张太太，叫她"太太"，我太太
2.	嫁	jià	V	(of a woman) to marry　她嫁给他
3.	新婚	xīnhūn	V	to be newly married　新婚的丈夫和妻子
4.	幸福	xìngfú	A/N	happy; happiness　祝你幸福，幸福生活；今天的幸福
5.	政府	zhèngfǔ	N	government　中国政府，上海市政府
6.	登记	dēngjì	V	to register　结婚登记，去政府登记，去派出所登记
7.	结婚证	jiéhūnzhèng	N	marriage certificate　拿到结婚证
8.	喜糖	xǐtáng	N	wedding sweets (or candies)　发喜糖，请大家吃喜糖
9.	举行	jǔxíng	V	to hold (a meeting, ceremony, etc.)　举行展览，举行聚会，举行考试，举行纪念活动
10.	婚礼	hūnlǐ	N	wedding ceremony　举行婚礼，参加婚礼
11.	贴	tiē	V	to paste, to stick　贴邮票，贴照片
12.	红双喜字	hóng shuāngxǐ zì		red paper-cut of the character meaning "double happiness"　贴红双喜字
	双喜	shuāngxǐ	N	double happiness
	双	shuāng	A	double　双手，红双喜字
13.	新娘	xīnniáng	N	bride　做新娘，当新娘
14.	花轿	huājiào	N	bridal sedan chair　坐花轿，抬花轿
15.	宴席	yànxí	N	banquet, feast　摆宴席，结婚宴席，生日宴席
16.	客人	kèren	N	guest　请客人来，欢迎客人
17.	教堂	jiàotáng	N	church, cathedral　上教堂，在教堂举行婚礼
18.	亲戚	qīnqi	N	relative, kin　我的亲戚，我们是亲戚，亲戚朋友

19.	表姐	biǎojiě	N	elder female cousin
20.	只是	zhǐshì	Adv	just, merely　只是开个玩笑，不只是喝杯酒
21.	岳父	yuèfù	N	father-in-law (the wife's father)
22.	岳母	yuèmǔ	N	mother-in-law (the wife's mother)
23.	杰克	Jiékè	PN	Jack (name of an Australian)
24.	玉兰	Yùlán	PN	Yulan (name of a Chinese girl)

注释　Notes

① 婚礼热闹得很。

　　"The wedding ceremony is very jubilant."

　　The particle "得" and the adverb "很" are frequently used after adjectives and verbs indicating psychological activities. "A/V+得很" indicates a high degree. For example,

　　　　我们最近忙得很。

　　　　大家都高兴得很。

　　　　A：力波现在还想家吗？

　　　　B：他说还想得很。

② 说到宴席，我们只请亲戚朋友在一起喝杯酒。

　　"As for the wedding banquet, we only invite relatives and friends for a drink."

　　"说到+NP/VP/S-PP" indicates concerning somebody or something. It is used to bring up a topic and comment on it. For example,

　　　　说到学习成绩，我认为小田是我们班的第一名。

　　　　说到在饭馆买单，我们喜欢AA制。

　　　　说到杰克怎么称呼玉兰的父母，由他自己决定吧。

③ 你等着你岳父、岳母教你吧。

　　"Let your father-and mother-in-law give you advice about it."

　　A married man calls his wife's parents "岳父，岳母", and a married woman calls her husband's parents "公公，婆婆". However, in spoken Chinese, both men and women call their parents-in-law "爸爸，妈妈".

There are some other forms of address in this lesson. For example, children address their own parents as "老爸, 老妈". "太太" is a respectful form of address for married women, usually preceded by the surnames of their husbands, for example, "张太太", "王太太". When talking with other people, the husband can also call his wife "太太", as in "我太太". This usage is particularly common in China's Hong Kong, Macao, Taiwan, and other overseas Chinese communities. However, in China's mainland, the term "太太" fell out of use a long time ago and is now rarely used. (Most women in China's mainland do not use their husbands' surnames.) "姑爷" is a form of address for a man used by the senior members of his wife's family.

🎧 46 （二）

玉 兰：杰克，到了我家，见了我父母，你得叫爸、叫妈，记住了吗？

杰 克：记住了。你说得很容易，可是我怎么开得了口？

玉 兰：怎么开不了口？你跟着我叫吧。

杰 克：好，记住了。

*   *   *   *   *   *

玉 兰：爸、妈，我们回来了。最近我们忙得很，现在才有空儿回来看你们。

玉兰爸：哦，回来了就好。我跟你妈正在商量给你们办结婚宴席的事儿呢。

玉 兰：爸、妈，我们已经结婚好几个月了，④ 结婚宴席你们就别办了。再说……

玉兰爸：说什么咱们也得办。⑤ 这不是在你们北京城里，这是农村。

杰　克：先生，您听我们慢慢地说……

玉兰爸：什么？"先生"？你叫我"先生"？

玉　兰：杰克，我是怎么跟你说的？你说记住了，怎么又忘了？叫
　　　　"爸"，叫"爸"呀！老爸，杰克还不太习惯。说到我们俩结婚
　　　　的事儿，⑥ 现在得按新的办法办，您怎么还是老脑筋啊？⑦

玉兰妈：什么叫老脑筋？这是咱们的规矩。

杰　克：太太，您别生气……

玉兰妈：玉兰爸，你听，他叫我"太太"！

玉　兰：你得叫"妈"。妈，他还不懂我们的规矩。

玉兰妈：看得出来，他是不懂我们的规矩。你一个人跑到中国来，想
　　　　怎么做就怎么做，你们村里的人谁也看不见。

玉　兰：妈，您这就不明白了，他家不住在农村，他家在悉尼市里。

玉兰妈：哦，"在城里"。你们知道吗？结婚是一辈子的大事啊！什么
　　　　都没有结婚重要！不请亲戚朋友和邻居吃饭，你们胡同的人
　　　　不说你吗？⑧

杰　克：别说我们那条"胡同"，连我住的那一座楼里，也没有人会
　　　　批评我。跟您这么说吧，我们谁也不认识谁。

玉兰妈：可是我不能让村里人说我，说我女儿。

玉兰爸：我看就这么决定了：我们去饭馆里请
　　　　两个好厨师，在家里摆十几桌宴席。

除了亲戚朋友以外，把村里
的人也请来，大家高高兴兴
地喝几杯。

玉兰妈：对，就这样了。这事儿由我
们来办，一定得热热闹闹地
办，让大家也认识认识我们
家的外国姑爷。

生词 New Words

1. 开口	kāikǒu	VO	to open one's mouth, to start to say (something embarrassing) 没开口，难开口，开不了口，怎么开得了口
*口	kǒu	N	mouth
2. 商量	shāngliang	V	to consult, to talk over 商量这件事，商量这个问题，跟他商量，两个人商量，大家商量
3. 俩	liǎ	Nu-M	(coll.) two (people) 我们俩，他们俩，你们俩，咱俩
4. 脑筋	nǎojīn	N	brain, mind, way of thinking 脑筋好，动脑筋，老脑筋
5. 规矩	guīju	N	rule, established practice, custom 懂规矩，不懂我们的规矩
6. 生气	shēngqì	VO	to get angry 别生气，她还在生气，生我的气
7. 大事	dàshì	N	important event, major issue 国家大事，世界大事，一辈子的大事
8. 邻居	línjū	N	neighbor 好邻居，我们家的邻居，请邻居吃饭

9.	胡同	hútòng	N	lane, alley 北京的胡同，你们胡同，你们胡同的人，一条胡同
10.	批评	pīpíng	V	to criticize 批评我，批评这件事
11.	决定	juédìng	V/N	to decide; decision 决定结婚，决定请客，决定去黄山旅游，决定出发的时间，就这么决定了；作出决定
12.	厨师	chúshī	N	cook, chef 请两个好厨师
13.	姑爷	gūye	N	son-in-law 新姑爷，我们家的姑爷，外国姑爷
14.	悉尼	Xīní	PN	Sydney

补充生词 Supplementary Words

1.	导演	dǎoyǎn	N/V	director; to direct (a film, play, etc.)
2.	奇特	qítè	A	peculiar, unusual
3.	庆祝	qìngzhù	V	to celebrate
4.	王安石	Wáng Ānshí	PN	Wang Anshi (a well-known Chinese statesman and writer of the Song Dynasty)
5.	走马灯	zǒumǎdēng	N	running horse lantern—lantern with such rotating shadow figures as horses, etc.
	灯	dēng	N	lamp, lantern
6.	对联	duìlián	N	antithetical couplet
7.	上联	shànglián	N	first line of a couplet
8.	熄(灯)	xī (dēng)	V	to put out (a lamp)
9.	对	duì	V	to match
10.	下联	xiàlián	N	second line of a couplet
11.	旗子	qízi	N	flag, banner
12.	老虎	lǎohǔ	N	tiger

13.	飘扬	piāoyáng	V	to flutter
14.	飞虎旗	fēihǔqí	N	a banner with the pattern of a flying tiger on it
15.	卷	juǎn	V	to roll up
16.	藏	cáng	V	to hide
17.	中榜	zhòngbǎng	VO	to become a successful candidate or applicant in the imperial examination

注释 Notes

④ 我们已经结婚好几个月了。

"We have been married for several months."

When used before numeral-measure words or time words, "好几" means "several" or "many", as in 好几个, 好几十, 好几千, 好几万, 好几倍 and 好几年.

⑤ 说什么咱们也得办。

"We have to do it anyhow."

Literally, this sentence means "No matter what you say, we will do it."

⑥ 说到我们俩结婚的事儿……

"As for our marriage…"

"俩" is the colloquial expression for "两个", as in 咱俩, 你们俩, 他们俩. A measure word cannot be used after "俩". The following expression is incorrect: "他们俩个".

⑦ 您怎么还是老脑筋啊?

"Why do you still get stuck in your old way of thinking?"

Here, "老" means "old", as in 老房子, 老光盘, 老电影. 脑筋 (literally, "brain") refers to one's point of view. "老脑筋" means "old way of thinking".

⑧ 你们胡同的人不说你吗?

"Wouldn't the people in your alley talk about (criticize) you?"

In Beijing dialect, "胡同" refers to a small street or alley. Here, the verb "说" means "reproach" or "criticize". For example,

他今天又来晚了，我说他了。

小马知道自己错了，别再说他了。

二、练习　Exercises

练习与运用　**Drills and Practice**　47

核心句 KEY SENTENCES

1. 说到宴席，我们只请亲戚朋友在一起喝杯酒。
2. 最近我们忙得很。
3. 我们已经结婚好几个月了。
4. 说到我们俩结婚的事儿，现在得按新的办法办。
5. 我不能让村里人说我。

1. 熟读下列词组　Read the following phrases until you learn them by heart

（1）不算晚　　不算高　　　不算是谦虚　不算是决定　不算是批评
　　　算是很早　算是很大方　算是比赛　　算是访问　　算是检查

（2）好得很　　冷得很　　　安静得很　　年轻得很　　容易得很
　　　喜欢得很　放心得很　　担心得很　　关心得很　　习惯得很

（3）说到他们俩　　说到中国画　　　说到安静　　　说到艰苦朴素
　　　说到游览黄山　说到贷款买汽车　说到谁来买单　说到工作认真

（4）好几万　　好几十万　　好几百万　　好几千万　　好几亿
　　　好几天　　好几个星期　好几个月　　好几十年　　好几个世纪
　　　好几首诗　好几篇课文　好几百块钱　好几十棵树　好几千辆车

2. 句型替换 Pattern drills

（1）A：你们<u>结婚</u>，还得<u>摆宴席</u>吧？

B：是啊。说到<u>摆宴席</u>，<u>我们只请亲戚朋友在一起喝杯酒</u>。

上大学	参加考试	实在不容易啊
举行纪念活动	作准备	我们买些东西就行了
去西藏旅游	事先检查身体	那两位八十多岁的老人有点儿担心

（2）A：他们已经<u>结婚</u>了吗？

B：他们已经<u>结婚</u> <u>好几个月</u>了。

登记	好几个星期
回家	好几天
退休	好几年

（3）A：他<u>身体</u>怎么样？

B：他<u>身体</u> <u>好</u>得很。

工作	辛苦
生活	节约
学习	困难
业余爱好	多

（4）A：这是<u>北京最小的胡同</u>吧？

B：这还不是<u>北京最小的胡同</u>，<u>那条胡同</u>比这<u>小</u>多了。

你们家最好看的花儿	那盆君子兰	好看
你们班最高的成绩	小谢的成绩	高
你们那儿最新的饭店	长安饭店	新

3. 课堂活动 Classroom activity

One student uses "说到……" to introduce a topic of conversation. Other students join the conversation to express their opinions about the topic. For example,

A：说到贷款买汽车，

B：我认为小云的看法是对的。

C：小云的妈妈是老脑筋。

D：我是做不到的。

…… ……

4. 会话练习 Conversation practice

会话常用语 IDIOMATIC EXPRESSIONS IN CONVERSATION

我想说的不是这个意思 (This is not what I'm talking about.)

我是说 (What I'm saying is...)

怎么开得了口 (How can I say that? /How can I open my mouth?)

我是怎么跟你说的 (What did I tell you?)

我看就这么决定了 (I think we'll settle it this way.)

【祝贺新婚　Congratulating the newly-weds】

A：听说你们快要结婚了，什么时候请我们吃喜糖?

B：我们打算下个月旅行结婚。

A：祝你们新婚快乐，生活幸福!

B：谢谢! 等我们旅行回来，还要请你们喝喜酒。

【澄清观点　Clarifying one's point of view】

A：你是说这部电影故事不够复杂?

B：我不是这个意思。我是说演员演得太简单了，没有把主要角色的复杂关系演好。

A：你是不是认为演员是这部电影的主要问题?

B：演员还不算是主要问题。我的意思是导演（dǎoyǎn）水平不高。

【劝慰 Comforting or consoling】

A：什么？她说我是老脑筋，跟不上时代了？

B：她不是这个意思，您别生气。您听我慢慢儿说。

A：我不听。让她把话说清楚，是怎么回事儿。

B：她不了解这件事儿，所以她说得很不合适。您不要为这件事儿生气。

【决定 Making a decision】

A：听说你要回国了？

B：是啊。我家里有点儿事儿，我决定下星期就回国。

A：那你就参加不了考试了。你再好好儿地想一想吧。

B：下下星期才考试，我等不了那么长的时间。我一定要在15号以前
到家。没有别的办法，就这么决定了。

A：好吧，那就这样吧。

5. 看图说话 Describe the following picture

6. 交际练习 Communication exercises

(1) Describe the wedding customs in your country.

　　After you speak, write down what you have said.

(2) Write a greeting card to your friend who are going to have their wedding.

阅读与复述 Reading Comprehension and Paraphrasing

🎧 48　奇特（qítè）的红双喜字

中国人举行婚礼时常用红纸写一个大"囍"字，贴在门上，表示庆祝（qìngzhù）。

传说这个红双喜字最早是宋代文学家王安石（Wáng Ānshí）写出来的。王安石在去京城参加考试的路上，看见一家门口挂着一个很大的走马灯（zǒumǎdēng），上边写着一副对联（duìlián）的上联（shànglián）："走马灯，灯走马，灯熄（xī）马停步。"希望有人能对（duì）出下联（xiàlián）。王安石看完了就说："这是一副很好的上联！"一位站在走马灯旁边的老人忙对他说："先生，您请进！"王安石回答说："对不起，我要去京城参加考试，现在没有时间。等回来的时候，我一定给您对出下联。"

考完试，王安石觉得自己考得很不错，心里很高兴。在回来的路上，他看见一面旗子（qízi），旗子上画着一只老虎（lǎohǔ），在风中飘扬（piāoyáng）。他想，用飞虎旗（fēihǔqí）去对走马灯，不是很好吗？他一边走一边念：

走马灯，灯走马，灯熄马停步。

飞虎旗，旗飞虎，旗卷（juǎn）虎藏（cáng）身。

一会儿，王安石又来到了那家人的门前。那位老人看见他来了，就非常高兴地走上去说："先生，您来了，请进！请进！"

王安石对老人说："不用进去了，我已经对出来了。我的下联是：'飞虎旗，旗飞虎，旗卷虎藏身。'""太好了！太好了！有人对出来了！"那位老人一边大声地说着，一边跑进屋去告诉小姐。小姐听了，笑了笑。

老人又走出来问王安石："先生，您结婚了没有？"

"还没有。"王安石说。

这时，老人才对王安石说："上联是我们家小姐出的。如果哪位没有结婚的年轻人对上了，我们家小姐就嫁给他。您的下联对得很好，我们家小姐很高兴。现在，只要您愿意，您就是我们家的姑爷了。"王安石想，这位小姐一定读过很多书，就决定跟她结婚。

就在王安石举行婚礼的那天，他收到了中榜（zhòngbǎng）的通知。两件喜事一起到来，他高兴极了，就用一张红纸写了这么一个奇特的"囍"字，贴在门上。

后来，人们结婚的时候，都习惯在门上贴一个大红双喜字。

三、语法复习　Grammar Review

1 几种补语　Types of complements

（1）情态补语　Modal complement

你来得真早。

他做中国菜做得很好吃。

他汉字写得很漂亮。

汉语他说得不太流利。

他玩儿得很高兴。

他们忙得没有时间唱京剧。

外边安静得听不见一点儿声音。

他累得头疼。

（2）程度补语　Complement of degree

昨天热极了。

上海的东西比这儿便宜多了。

他最近忙得很。

（3）结果补语　Resultative complement

她戴上了那条围巾。

他们没有把礼物打开。

他没有找着火车票。

我记住了那位作家说的话。

（4）可能补语　Complement of possibility

他今天做得完这些练习。

我看不见那棵树。

他们听不懂上海话。

汽车开不进来。

这么多东西，他拿不上来。

小孩儿吃得了这么多水果吗？

车里坐不下这么多人。

我们搬得动这张大床。

2　疑问代词活用　Flexible usages of interrogative pronouns

（1）表示反问　Indicating a question asked in retort

谁说他不去？

她哪儿有钱买车呢？

他什么没吃过？什么没见过？

他怎么没有来？他来了。

（2）表示虚指　Indicating indefinite reference

你想喝点儿什么吗？

我不记得谁给你打过电话。

我好像在哪儿见过他。

（3）表示任指　Indicating arbitrary reference

这么好的京剧，谁都想看。

他什么也不想吃。

她哪儿也不愿意去。

哪种方法都不行。

他怎么记也记不住。

The same pronoun can also be used twice to indicate arbitrary reference.

我们楼里谁也不认识谁。

谁知道这个词的意思谁就回答。

你一个人想怎么做就怎么做。

你做什么我就吃什么。

哪儿好玩儿就去哪儿。

3 副词"再"和"又"　The adverbs "再" and "又"

副词"再"　The adverb "再"

（1）表示将要重复　Indicating somebody will do something again

请再说一遍。

我们再聊一会儿吧。

他说他明天再来。

我以后不再去了。

（2）表示动作将在某一时间或情况以后发生　Indicating that an action will occur some time or under certain condition

我们先翻译生词，再复习课文。

吃完饭再走吧。

副词 "又"　The adverb "又"

（1）表示已经重复　Indicating repetition

你上星期已经参观了一次，怎么今天又去参观了？

他昨天没有来，今天又没有来。

（2）表示有所补充　Indicating supplementation

我昨天去了商店，又看了电影。

他没有去上课，又没有好好儿复习，所以考得很不好。

（3）表示同时存在的情况　Indicating coexistent situations

他们又唱又跳。

这个姑娘又年轻又漂亮。

（4）表示两件矛盾的事情或情况　Indicating two contradictory things or situations

她很怕冷，又不愿意多穿衣服。

我很想跟你聊聊，可是又怕你没有时间。

四、字与词　Chinese Characters and Words

区别多音多义字
Distinguish polyphonic and polysemic Chinese characters

　　Among the 3,500 commonly-used Chinese characters, 11% of them are polyphonic and polysemic ones. For example, "还" has two pronunciations. When used as an adverb, it is pronounced "hái", as in "还有，还想"; when used as a verb, it is pronounced "huán", as in "还书，还贷款". "好" also has two pronunciations. One is "hǎo", as in "好书，好地方", and the other, "hào" as in "爱好". The meanings expressed by the different pronunciations are completely different, so we need to distinguish them when we learn Chinese characters.

Marriage Customs in China

There are many ethnic groups in China, resulting in various kinds of marriage customs, among which the traditional wedding ceremony of the Han ethnic group is an important part of the Chinese marriage culture.

Ancient Chinese believed that dusk was the auspicious moment of the day, so most weddings were held at dusk. The wedding ceremony, only next to the adulthood ceremony, is the second milestone in one's life. It can be divided into three stages: the pre-wedding ceremony (being engaged), the wedding ceremony (being married) and the post-wedding ceremony (being a son/daughter-in-law), with the first two being the major parts. Every stage has its own complicated procedures to go through. For example, both families would first get together to decide on the date of the wedding, and then the prospective groom's family is supposed to send betrothal presents to the bride-to-be's family and the bride-to-be's family should prepare a dowry. On the wedding day, the groom is supposed to go fetch the bride and then the wedding ceremony is held. Nowadays, many of the complicated procedures have been simplified, except in a few places where an engagement is still required before the wedding and the newly-weds need to visit the bride's family three days after the wedding.

At a traditional Chinese wedding, the bride's head was covered with a square red veil, commonly referred to as "盖头", so that the bride wouldn't feel embarrassed and the groom wouldn't see the bride's face until they were truly married. A bridal sedan chair used to be a must for a groom to fetch his bride. The special sedan chair was often gorgeously decorated and painted red, symbolizing happiness and auspiciousness. People today no longer use bridal sedan chairs, but for many brides, they won't feel like really getting married unless they take a bridal car to the groom's home. The bridal car, often decorated with flowers, is actually a modern version of the traditional bridal sedan.

Now, more and more Chinese people tend to have a wedding with the Chinese and Western styles blended together. Usually, the bride and groom are dressed in Western-style wedding dresses during the ceremony, which is presided over by the chief witness. Then they change into Chinese-style wedding dresses for dinner and reception.

Now that you have finished Books 1~3 of *New Practical Chinese Reader*, you should have learned over 1,900 elementary words, of which 1,500 are required to master, plus over 1,000 Chinese characters, the basic grammatical items and 300 key sentences. You can express your ideas about topics in daily life and certain social issues and communicate with other people. With the help of a dictionary, you can also read simple essays.

Congratulations on having completed the initial stage of your study of Chinese.

Book 4 of *New Practical Chinese Reader* will guide youinthe intermediate stage of Chinese learning.

附录 Appendices

语法术语缩略形式一览表
Abbreviations for Grammar Terms

Abbreviations	Grammar Terms in English	Grammar Terms in Chinese	Grammar Terms in *pinyin*
A	Adjective	形容词	xíngróngcí
Adv	Adverb	副词	fùcí
AP	Adjectival Phrase	形容词词组	xíngróngcí cízǔ
AsPt	Aspect Particle	动态助词	dòngtài zhùcí
Coll	Colloquial Expression	口语词语	kǒuyǔ cíyǔ
Conj	Conjunction	连词	liáncí
IE	Idiomatic Expression	习惯用语	xíguàn yòngyǔ
Int	Interjection	叹词	tàncí
M	Measure Word	量词	liàngcí
MdPt	Modal Particle	语气助词	yǔqì zhùcí
N	Noun	名词	míngcí
NP	Noun Phrase	名词词组	míngcí cízǔ
Nu	Numeral	数词	shùcí
Nu-MP	Numeral-Measure Word Phrase	数量词组	shùliàng cízǔ
O	Object	宾语	bīnyǔ
Ono	Onomatopoeia	象声词	xiàngshēngcí
OpV	Optative Verb	能愿动词	néngyuàn dòngcí
P	Predicate	谓语	wèiyǔ
PN	Proper Noun	专有名词	zhuānyǒu míngcí
Pr	Pronoun	代词	dàicí
Pref	Prefix	词头	cítóu
Prep	Preposition	介词	jiècí
Pt	Particle	助词	zhùcí
PW	Place Word	地点词	dìdiǎncí
QPr	Question Pronoun	疑问代词	yíwèn dàicí
QPt	Question Particle	疑问助词	yíwèn zhùcí
S	Subject	主语	zhǔyǔ
S-PP	Structural-Predicate Phrase	主谓词组	zhǔwèi cízǔ
StPt	Structural Particle	结构助词	jiégòu zhùcí
Suf	Suffix	词尾	cíwěi
TW	Time Word	时间词	shíjiāncí
V	Verb	动词	dòngcí
VC	Verb plus Complement	动补式动词	dòngbǔshì dòngcí
VO	Verb plus Object	动宾式动词	dòngbīnshì dòngcí
VP	Verbal Phrase	动词词组	dòngcí cízǔ

生词索引（简繁对照）
Vocabulary Index

(Simplified Chinese Characters vs Traditional Chinese Characters)

词条	繁体	拼音	词性	英译	课号
A					
AA制	AA制	AA zhì	N	to go Dutch	37
爱好者	愛好者	àihàozhě	N	lover (of art, sports, etc.), enthusiast	30
安静	安静	ānjìng	A	quiet	27
按	按	àn	Prep	according to	37
按时	按時	ànshí	Adv	timely, on time	35
澳门	澳門	Àomén	PN	Macao	31
B					
坝	壩	bà	N	dam	34
摆	擺	bǎi	V	to put, to place	29
班	班	bān	N	class	37
搬	搬	bān	V	to move	27
办法	辦法	bànfǎ	N	way, method	32
棒	棒	bàng	A	(*coll.*) awesome	32
包	包	bāo	N	bag, satchel	32
包括	包括	bāokuò	V	to include	31
宝	寶	bǎo	N	treasure	28
保护	保護	bǎohù	V	to protect	33

杯（子）	杯（子）	bēi (zi)	N	cup	28
背	背	bēi	V	to carry	32
背包	背包	bēibāo	N	knapsack, backpack	32
背	背	bèi	V	to recite, to learn by heart	36
倍	倍	bèi	M	time, fold	35
比较	比較	bǐjiào	Adv/V	comparatively, quite; to compare	29
比如	比如	bǐrú	V	to give an example	27
比上不足，比下有余	比上不足，比下有餘	bǐ shàng bùzú, bǐ xià yǒuyú	IE	better than some, though not as good as others	32
变	變	biàn	V	to change	35
表姐	表姐	biǎojiě	N	elder female cousin	38
表示	表示	biǎoshì	V/N	to express; expression	28
别人	别人	biéren	Pr	other people	28
饼	餅	bǐng	N	cake	28
病	病	bìng	V/N	to fall ill; disease	30
不必	不必	búbì	Adv	not necessarily	29
不过	不過	búguò	Conj	however, but	28
不如	不如	bùrú	V	to be not as good as, to be inferior to	29
步	步	bù	M	step	33

C

草原	草原	cǎoyuán	N	grassland	36
叉（子）	叉（子）	chā (zi)	N	fork	27
茶馆	茶館	cháguǎn	N	teahouse	27
差不多	差不多	chàbuduō	A/Adv	about the same; almost	32
长江	長江	Cháng Jiāng	PN	the Changjiang River (or Yangtze River)	31
场所	場所	chǎngsuǒ	N	place	27

称	稱	chēng	V	to call	32
称呼	稱呼	chēnghu	V/N	to call; a form of address	32
称赞	稱讚	chēngzàn	V	to praise, to compliment	28
成绩	成績	chéngjì	N	test result	31
出汗	出汗	chū hàn	V O	to sweat	30
除了······以外	除了······以外	chúle······yǐwài		except, besides	36
厨师	厨師	chúshī	N	cook, chef	38
传说	傳説	chuánshuō	N	legend	34
船	船	chuán	N	boat, ship	34
床前明月光	床前明月光	Chuáng qián míng yuè guāng		In front of the bed, the bright moonlight shines.	36
春节	春節	Chūn Jié	PN	Spring Festival, Chinese New Year	28
凑合	凑合	còuhe	V	(*coll.*) to make do, to be passable, to be not too bad	32

D

*打	打	dǎ	V	to beat	30
大方	大方	dàfang	A	generous	37
大陆	大陸	Dàlù	PN	the mainland (of China)	31
大事	大事	dàshì	N	important event, major issue	38
贷	貸	dài	V	to borrow or to lend	35
贷款	貸款	dàikuǎn	VO/N	to provide or to ask for a loan; loan	35
戴	戴	dài	V	to put on, to wear	28
担心	擔心	dānxīn	VO	to worry	28
单	單	dān	N	list	37
刀（子）	刀（子）	dāo (zi)	N	knife	27

刀叉	刀叉	dāochā	N	knife and fork	27
得到	得到	dédào	V	to get	28
地	地	de	Pt	*used to form an adverbial adjunct*	29
登	登	dēng	V	to publish (an essay, article, etc.)	33
登记	登記	dēngjì	V	to register	38
低头思	低頭思	Dī tóu sī		(I) lower my head and think of (my)	
故乡	故鄉	gùxiāng		beloved hometown.	36
地道	地道	dìdao	A	pure, typical, genuine	32
地理	地理	dìlǐ	N	geography	31
弟子	弟子	dìzǐ	N	disciple, student	29
弟子不必	弟子不必	dìzǐ búbì	IE	Disciples are not necessarily inferior	
不如师	不如師	bùrú shī		to their teachers.	29
点心	點心	diǎnxin	N	refreshments, pastry	27
丢人	丟人	diūrén	VO	to lose face, to be disgraced	35
东北	東北	Dōngběi	PN	the Northeast	36
动	動	dòng	V	to move	36
动作	動作	dòngzuò	N	movement, action	30
都市	都市	dūshì	N	big city, metropolis	33
读	讀	dú	V	to read, to study	32
读书	讀書	dúshū	VO	to study, to read a book	32
杜甫	杜甫	Dù Fǔ	PN	Du Fu (a great poet of the Tang Dynasty)	
					36
对面	對面	duìmiàn	N	opposite side	30

E

| 俄罗斯 | 俄羅斯 | Éluósī | PN | Russia | 31 |

F

发现	發現	fāxiàn	V	to find	27
饭店	飯店	fàndiàn	N	hotel	37
方式	方式	fāngshì	N	way	30
非洲	非洲	Fēizhōu	PN	Africa	33
……分之……	……分之……	……fēn zhī……		*used to express a fraction, percentage*	35
风俗	風俗	fēngsú	N	custom	27
封	封	fēng	M	*a measure word for letters*	36
疯	瘋	fēng	V	to be mad, to be crazy	35
服务	服務	fúwù	V	to serve	27
服务员	服務員	fúwùyuán	N	waiter/waitress	27
父	父	fù		father	32
父母	父母	fùmǔ	N	father and mother, parents	32
付	付	fù	V	to pay	35
复杂	複雜	fùzá	A	complicated	36

G

干	乾	gān	A	dry	28
干杯	乾杯	gānbēi	VO	to drink a toast	28
干净	乾净	gānjìng	A	clean	27
感觉	感覺	gǎnjué	N/V	feeling; to feel	31
感谢	感謝	gǎnxiè	V	to thank	28
橄榄球	橄欖球	gǎnlǎnqiú	N	rugby, American football	37
高明	高明	gāomíng	A	brilliant, wise	29
高新技术	高新技術	gāoxīn jìshù		high technology	32

高原	高原	gāoyuán	N	plateau, highland	33
搞	搞	gǎo	V	to engage in	32
个人	個人	gèrén	N	individual (person)	32
各	各	gè	Pr	each, every	36
跟	跟	gēn	V	to follow	35
更	更	gèng	Adv	more	27
工资	工資	gōngzī	N	salary	32
公里	公里	gōnglǐ	M	kilometer	31
够	够	gòu	V/Adv	to be adequate; enough, sufficiently	32
姑爷	姑爺	gūye	N	son-in-law	38
古	古	gǔ	A	ancient	29
古迹	古迹	gǔjì	N	historical sites	31
古书	古書	gǔshū	N	ancient book	29
鼓	鼓	gǔ	N	drum	30
刮	颳	guā	V	to blow	34
挂	挂	guà	V	to hang	29
关系	關係	guānxì	N	relation, relationship	33
关心	關心	guānxīn	V	to be concerned with	32
观念	觀念	guānniàn	N	concept	35
管	管	guǎn	V	to bother about, to mind	35
规矩	規矩	guīju	N	rule, established practice, custom	38
国土	國土	guótǔ	N	land	31

H

海	海	hǎi	N	sea	31
寒带	寒帶	hándài	N	frigid zone	36
好处	好處	hǎochu	N	benefit	35

好看	好看	hǎokàn	A	pleasant to look at, good-looking	29
好奇	好奇	hàoqí	A	curious	32
河	河	hé	N	river	31
红双喜字	紅雙喜字	hóng shuāngxǐ zì		red paper-cut of the character meaning "double happiness"	38
后来	後來	hòulái	N	afterwards, later	30
胡同	胡同	hútòng	N	lane, alley	38
壶	壺	hú	N	kettle, pot	27
湖北	湖北	Húběi	PN	a province in central China with its capital in Wuhan	34
湖南	湖南	Húnán	PN	a province of China in the south of the middle reaches of the Yangtze River with its capital in Changsha	34
互相	互相	hùxiāng	Adv	mutually, each other	29
*花	花	huā	V	to spend	32
花轿	花轎	huājiào	N	bridal sedan chair	38
欢迎	歡迎	huānyíng	V	to welcome	29
环境	環境	huánjìng	N	environment	33
黄河	黃河	Huáng Hé	PN	the Yellow River	31
黄山	黃山	Huáng Shān	PN	Mt. Huang	31
回	回	huí	M	*a measure word used for happenings or events*	37
婚礼	婚禮	hūnlǐ	N	wedding ceremony	38
活	活	huó	V	to live	33
活动	活動	huódòng	V/N	to exercise; activity	30

J ....

| 积蓄 | 積蓄 | jīxù | N/V | savings; to save | 35 |

*纪念	紀念	jìniàn	V	to commemorate	28, 33
纪念品	紀念品	jìniànpǐn	N	souvenir	28
季	季	jì	N	season	36
季节	季節	jìjié	N	season	36
既…… 又……	既…… 又……	jì……yòu……		both … and …	33
继续	繼續	jìxù	V	to continue	33
*家	家	jiā	Suf	specialist in a certain field	29
家书抵 万金	家書抵 萬金	Jiāshū dǐ wàn jīn		A letter from home is worthy of ten thousand pieces of gold.	36
嫁	嫁	jià	V	(of a woman) to marry	38
艰苦	艱苦	jiānkǔ	A	arduous, hard	35
简单	簡單	jiǎndān	A	simple	30
建立	建立	jiànlì	V	to set up, to establish	33
剑	劍	jiàn	N	sword	30
江南	江南	Jiāngnán	PN	south of the Changjiang River	36
讲	講	jiǎng	V	to tell, to explain, to speak	34
浇	澆	jiāo	V	to water	29
叫做	叫做	jiàozuò	V	to be called	30
教堂	教堂	jiàotáng	N	church, cathedral	38
教育	教育	jiàoyù	V/N	to educate; education	33
接受	接受	jiēshòu	V	to accept	33
接着	接着	jiēzhe	V	to follow, to carry on	37
街	街	jiē	N	street	30
街心花园	街心花園	jiēxīn huāyuán		street garden	30
节日	節日	jiérì	N	festival	28
节约	節約	jiéyuē	V	to save, to economize	35

杰克	傑克	Jiékè	PN	Jack (name of an Australian)	38
结婚	結婚	jiéhūn	VO	to marry	32
结婚证	結婚證	jiéhūnzhèng	N	marriage certificate	38
解决	解決	jiějué	V	to solve	33
借债	借債	jièzhài	VO	to borrow money	35
巾	巾	jīn	N	a piece of cloth (used as a towel, scarf, kerchief, etc.)	28
金（子）	金（子）	jīn (zi)	N	gold	35
金钱	金錢	jīnqián	N	money	35
近	近	jìn	A	near, close	33
经济	經濟	jīngjì	N	economy	35
惊	驚	jīng	V	to surprise	28
惊喜	驚喜	jīngxǐ	N	pleasant surprise	28
敬酒	敬酒	jìng jiǔ	V O	to propose a toast	37
静	静	jìng	A	quiet	27
久	久	jiǔ	A	long (time)	34
酒杯	酒杯	jiǔbēi	N	wine glass/cup	37
就是	就是	jiùshì	Conj	*used for emphasis*	35
举	舉	jǔ	V	to hold up, to raise	37
举头望明月	舉頭望明月	Jǔ tóu wàng míng yuè		(I) raise (my) head and gaze at the bright moon.	36
举行	舉行	jǔxíng	V	to hold (a meeting, ceremony, etc.)	38
句	句	jù	M	*used of language*	29
句子	句子	jùzi	N	sentence	29
决定	決定	juédìng	V/N	to decide; decision	38
绝对	絕對	juéduì	Adv	absolutely	35
君子兰	君子蘭	jūnzǐlán	N	kaffir lily	29

K

咖啡馆	咖啡館	kāfēiguǎn	N	cafe, coffee bar	27
开花儿	開花兒	kāihuār	VO	to bloom	29
开口	開口	kāikǒu	VO	to open one's mouth, to start to say (something embarrassing)	38
看法	看法	kànfǎ	N	view	27
看见	看見	kànjiàn	VC	to see, to catch sight of	33
烤全羊	烤全羊	kǎoquányáng	N	roasted whole lamb	37
靠近	靠近	kàojìn	V	to draw near, to approach	33
科学	科學	kēxué	N	science	33
科学家	科學家	kēxuéjiā	N	scientist	33
棵	棵	kē	M	*a measure word for plants*	31
可	可	kě	Adv	*used for emphasis*	34
可乐	可樂	kělè	N	coke or soft drink similar to Coca-Cola	34
客人	客人	kèren	N	guest	38
空气	空氣	kōngqì	N	air	33
*口	口	kǒu	N	mouth	38
块	塊	kuài	M	piece, lump	27
筷子	筷子	kuàizi	N	chopsticks	27
款	款	kuǎn	N	money	35
困难	困難	kùnnan	A/N	difficult; difficulty	35

L

辣	辣	là	A	hot, spicy	34
来往	來往	láiwǎng	V	to come and go	34

老人	老人	lǎorén	N	senior citizen, elderly man or woman	30
礼轻情意重	禮輕情意重	lǐ qīng qíngyì zhòng	IE	A small gift means a great deal.	28
李白	李白	Lǐ Bái	PN	Li Bai (name of a great Chinese poet of the Tang Dynasty)	34
立交桥	立交橋	lìjiāoqiáo	N	overpass	30
俩	倆	liǎ	Nu-M	(*coll.*) two (people)	38
连	連	lián	Conj	even	34
练	練	liàn	V	to practice	29
凉	涼	liáng	A	cool, cold	34
凉快	涼快	liángkuai	A	cool	36
两岸猿声啼不住	兩岸猿聲啼不住	Liǎng àn yuán shēng tí bú zhù		the monkeys on both banks are still gibbering	34
聊天儿	聊天兒	liáotiānr	VO	to chat	27
了	了	liǎo	V	(*used in conjunction with* 得 *or* 不 *after a verb*) can	36
了解	瞭解	liǎojiě	V	to get to know, to find out	27
邻居	鄰居	línjū	N	neighbor	38
灵山	靈山	Líng Shān	PN	Mt. Ling (a mountain in the suburbs of Beijing)	33
留学	留學	liúxué	VO	to study abroad	32
路线	路綫	lùxiàn	N	route, itinerary	36
旅游	旅游	lǚyóu	V	to tour	31
绿化	綠化	lùhuà	V	to make (a place) green by planting trees; to afforest	33
锣	鑼	luó	N	gong	30

M

买单	買單	mǎidān	V	(*coll.*) to pay a bill	37
毛	毛	máo	N	hair, feather, down	28
毛笔	毛筆	máobǐ	N	writing brush	28
美丽	美麗	měilì	A	beautiful	32
门口	門口	ménkǒu	N	doorway	30
蒙族	蒙族	Měngzú	PN	Mongolian ethnic group	37
梦	夢	mèng	N	dream	35
梦话	夢話	mènghuà	N	words uttered in one's sleep, nonsense	35
迷	迷	mí	V	to be fascinated	34
米	米	mǐ	M	meter	31
		mǐ	N	rice	35
面积	面積	miànjī	N	area	31
民歌	民歌	míngē	N	folk song	37
民间	民間	mínjiān	N	folk	30
名不虚传	名不虛傳	míng bù xū chuán	IE	to deserve the reputation	32
名牌	名牌	míngpái	N	famous brand	28
名胜	名勝	míngshèng	N	scenic spots	31
名胜古迹	名勝古迹	míngshèng gǔjì	IE	scenic spots and historical sites	31
明白	明白	míngbai	V/A	to understand; clear, explicit	37
母	母	mǔ		mother	31
母亲	母親	mǔqīn	N	mother	31
木（头）	木（頭）	mù (tou)		wood	33
木屋	木屋	mùwū	N	log cabin	33

N

那么	那麼	nàme	Pr	so, like that	28
脑筋	腦筋	nǎojīn	N	brain, mind, way of thinking	38
闹	鬧	nào	A/V	noisy; to make a noise/racket	27
内蒙	内蒙	Nèiměng	PN	Inner Mongolia	36
扭	扭	niǔ	V	to twist, to turn	30
扭秧歌	扭秧歌	niǔ yāngge	V O	to do the *yangge* dance	30
暖气	暖氣	nuǎnqì	N	heating	36

O

| 哦 | 哦 | ò | Int | oh, aha (*expressing a sudden realization*) | 32 |

P

怕	怕	pà	V	to fear, to be afraid of	34
牌（子）	牌（子）	pái (zi)	N	brand	28
盘	盤	pán	M	dish	27
盘子	盤子	pánzi	N	plate, dish	27
跑步	跑步	pǎobù	VO	to jog	30
盆	盆	pén	N	a container made of plastic or clay for growing plants in	29
盆景	盆景	pénjǐng	N	miniature trees and rockery in a pot, bonsai	29
批评	批評	pīpíng	V	to criticize	38
啤酒	啤酒	píjiǔ	N	beer	28
品	品	pǐn	Suf	article, product	28
平方	平方	píngfāng	M	square	31

平方公里	平方公里	píngfāng gōnglǐ	M	square kilometer	31
朴素	樸素	pǔsù	A	simple, plain	35

Q

其余	其餘	qíyú	Pr	the remainder, the rest	35
奇怪	奇怪	qíguài	A	strange, odd	31
企业	企業	qǐyè	N	enterprise	32
气候	氣候	qìhòu	N	climate	36
谦虚	謙虛	qiānxū	A	modest	29
墙	墙	qiáng	N	wall	29
抢	搶	qiǎng	V	to snatch, to make efforts to be the first, to fight for	37
敲	敲	qiāo	V	to beat, to knock (at/on sth.)	30
敲锣打鼓	敲鑼打鼓	qiāo luó dǎ gǔ	IE	to beat drums and gongs	30
桥	橋	qiáo	N	bridge	30
巧	巧	qiǎo	A	by chance, coincidental, skillful	32
切	切	qiē	V	to cut, to slice	27
亲戚	親戚	qīnqi	N	relative, kin	38
勤俭	勤儉	qínjiǎn	A	hard-working and thrifty	35
轻	輕	qīng	A	light	28
轻舟已过万重山	輕舟已過万重山	Qīng zhōu yǐ guò wàn chóng shān		the boat has flown away past tens of thousands of hills	34
清楚	清楚	qīngchu	A	clear	32
情意	情意	qíngyì	N	affection	28
请客	請客	qǐngkè	VO	to invite sb. to dinner, usually with the intention to pay	37
球场	球場	qiúchǎng	N	ground or court for ball games	37

| 确实 | 確實 | quèshí | Adv | really, indeed | 33 |
| 裙子 | 裙子 | qúnzi | N | skirt | 36 |

R

然后	然後	ránhòu	Conj	then, after that	37
热带	熱帶	rèdài	N	torrid zone, tropics	36
热闹	熱鬧	rènao	A/V	bustling with noise and excitement; to liven up	27
人口	人口	rénkǒu	N	population	31
人们	人們	rénmen	N	people	29
认为	認為	rènwéi	V	to think, to consider	32
日出	日出	rì chū		sunrise	34
日子	日子	rìzi	N	day, life	35
入	入	rù	V	to enter, to go in/into	27
入乡随俗	入鄉隨俗	rù xiāng suí sú	IE	When in Rome, do as the Romans do; to conform to local customs	27

S

三峡	三峡	Sānxiá	PN	the Three Gorges (of the Yangtze River)	34
沙漠	沙漠	shāmò	N	desert	33
莎士比亚	莎士比亞	Shāshìbǐyà	PN	William Shakespeare	36
山峰	山峰	shānfēng	N	peak	31
山水	山水	shānshuǐ	N	mountain and water, landscape	34
山水画	山水畫	shānshuǐhuà	N	landscape painting	34
商量	商量	shāngliang	V	to consult, to talk over	38

商品	商品	shāngpǐn	N	commodity, goods	35
商品经济	商品經濟	shāngpǐn jīngjì		commodity economy	35
赏	賞	shǎng	V	to enjoy	28
上班	上班	shàngbān	VO	to go to work	30
稍	稍	shāo	Adv	slightly, a little	27
什么的	什麼的	shénmede	Pt	(*coll.*) and so on	32
神女峰	神女峰	Shénnǚ Fēng	PN	Shennü Peak	34
生病	生病	shēngbìng	VO	to fall ill	30
生产	生產	shēngchǎn	V	to produce	35
生命	生命	shēngmìng	N	life	35
生气	生氣	shēngqì	VO	to get angry	38
声	聲	shēng	N	sound, voice	27
声音	聲音	shēngyīn	N	sound, voice	27
师	師	shī	Suf	person skillful at a certain profession, expert, master	29
师不必贤于弟子	師不必賢于弟子	shī búbì xián yú dìzǐ	IE	Teachers are not necessarily wiser than their disciples	29
诗	詩	shī	N	poem	34
诗人	詩人	shīrén	N	poet	36
时代	時代	shídài	N	times, era	35
实现	實現	shíxiàn	V	to realize	35
食	食	shí	V	to eat	27
食物	食物	shíwù	N	food	27
世纪	世紀	shìjì	N	century	35
世界	世界	shìjiè	N	world	31
市	市	shì	N	city, municipality	33
事先	事先	shìxiān	N	in advance, beforehand	37

收	收	shōu	V	to receive, to accept	28
手	手	shǒu	N	hand	27
手指	手指	shǒuzhǐ	N	finger	27
首	首	shǒu	M	*a measure word for poems and songs, etc.*	34
首都	首都	shǒudū	N	capital	33
首先	首先	shǒuxiān	Conj	first of all, firstly	37
受	受	shòu	V	to receive, to be subjected to	33, 37
书法	書法	shūfǎ	N	calligraphy	28
书法家	書法家	shūfǎjiā	N	calligrapher	29
书房	書房	shūfáng	N	study	29
书架	書架	shūjià	N	bookshelf	29
熟	熟	shú	A	familiar	36
树	樹	shù	N	tree	31
双	雙	shuāng	A	double	38
水果	水果	shuǐguǒ	N	fruit	28
说话	説話	shuōhuà	VO	to speak, to talk	27
四川	四川	Sìchuān	PN	a province in southwest China with its capital in Chengdu	34
松树	松樹	sōngshù	N	pine (tree)	31
俗	俗	sú		custom	27
算	算	suàn	V	to consider, to regard as	32
随	隨	suí	V	to follow	27

T

| 台 | 臺 | tái | | stage, platform | 27 |

台湾	臺灣	Táiwān	PN	Taiwan	31
抬	擡	tái	V	to carry	37
太极剑	太極劍	tàijíjiàn	N	*taiji* sword (a kind of traditional Chinese swordplay)	30
太太	太太	tàitai	N	Mrs., madam	38
唐代	唐代	Tángdài	PN	Tang Dynasty	29
《唐诗选》	《唐詩選》	Tángshī Xuǎn	PN	*Selected Tang Poems*	36
糖	糖	táng	N	sweets, candy	28
特色	特色	tèsè	N	characteristic, feature	28
添	添	tiān	V	to add, to increase	37
舔	舔	tiǎn	V	to lick	27
条件	條件	tiáojiàn	N	condition	33
跳	跳	tiào	V	to jump, to leap	30
跳舞	跳舞	tiàowǔ	VO	to dance	30
贴	貼	tiē	V	to paste, to stick	38
听见	聽見	tīngjiàn	VC	to hear	30
挺	挺	tǐng	Adv	(*coll.*) very, quite	35
退休	退休	tuìxiū	V	to retire	30

W

外交	外交	wàijiāo	N	diplomacy	33
外交官	外交官	wàijiāoguān	N	diplomat	33
晚饭	晚飯	wǎnfàn	N	supper, dinner	37
万	萬	wàn	Nu	ten thousand	31
网	網	wǎng	N	net	33
网吧	網吧	wǎngbā	N	Internet cafe, cybercafe	30

网络	網絡	wǎngluò	N	Internet	32
*围	圍	wéi	V	to enclose	28
		wéi	V	to surround	30
围巾	圍巾	wéijīn	N	scarf	28
伟大	偉大	wěidà	A	great	36
为	為	wèi	Prep	for	34
味道	味道	wèidao	N	taste, flavor	37
味儿	味兒	wèir	N	taste, flavor	34
文房四宝	文房四寶	wénfáng sìbǎo	IE	the four treasures of the study	28
文学家	文學家	wénxuéjiā	N	writer	29
稳定	穩定	wěndìng	A	stable	35
污染	污染	wūrǎn	V	to pollute	33
屋（子）	屋（子）	wū (zi)	N	house, room	33
武术	武術	wǔshù	N	martial arts	30
舞	舞	wǔ	N	dance	27
舞蹈	舞蹈	wǔdǎo	N	dance	30
舞台	舞臺	wǔtái	N	stage	27
物	物	wù		thing	27

X

西餐	西餐	xīcān	N	Western-style food (meal)	27
西王母	西王母	Xīwángmǔ	PN	Queen Mother of the West (a figure in Chinese mythology)	34
西藏	西藏	Xīzàng	PN	Tibet	31
希望	希望	xīwàng	V/N	to hope; hope	28
悉尼	悉尼	Xīní	PN	Sydney	38

喜	喜	xǐ		to be happy	28
喜糖	喜糖	xǐtáng	N	wedding sweets (or candies)	38
下棋	下棋	xiàqí	VO	to play chess	30
夏令营	夏令營	xiàlìngyíng	N	summer camp	33
贤	賢	xián		virtuous, able	29
现代	現代	xiàndài	N	modern	36
乡	鄉	xiāng	N	village	27
香港	香港	Xiānggǎng	PN	Hong Kong	31
享受	享受	xiǎngshòu	V	to enjoy	35
小时候	小時候	xiǎoshíhou	N	in one's childhood	36
小意思	小意思	xiǎoyìsi	N	small token of affection	28
笑话	笑話	xiàohua	N/V	joke; to make fun of (sb.)	37
欣赏	欣賞	xīnshǎng	V	to appreciate, to enjoy	32
新婚	新婚	xīnhūn	V	to be newly married	38
新疆	新疆	Xīnjiāng	PN	Xinjiang (an autonomous region of China)	37
新娘	新娘	xīnniáng	N	bride	38
信用	信用	xìnyòng	N	credit	35
幸福	幸福	xìngfú	A/N	happy; happiness	38
休闲	休閑	xiūxián	V	to have leisure	30
修整	修整	xiūzhěng	V	to prune, to trim	29
选择	選擇	xuǎnzé	V/N	to select; choice	36

Y

研究	研究	yánjiū	V	to study, to research	33
宴席	宴席	yànxí	N	banquet, feast	38

秧歌	秧歌	yāngge	N	*yangge* dance	30
羊肉	羊肉	yángròu	N	mutton	37
养	養	yǎng	V	to grow, to raise	29
摇篮	搖籃	yáolán	N	cradle	31
要不	要不	yàobù	Conj	otherwise, or else	30
叶（子）	葉（子）	yè (zi)	N	leaf	29
页	頁	yè	M	page	36
夜	夜	yè	N	night	34
医务室	醫務室	yīwùshì	N	clinic	34
一辈子	一輩子	yíbèizi	N	all one's life, one's lifetime	35
移	移	yí	V	to move	33
移植	移植	yízhí	V	to transplant	33
疑是地上霜	疑是地上霜	Yí shì dì shàng shuāng		(I) wonder if (it) is frost on the ground.	36
一般	一般	yìbān	A	general, ordinary	28
一边……一边……	一邊……一邊……	yìbiān……yìbiān……		at the same time, simultaneously	27
亿	億	yì	Nu	a hundred million	31
艺术	藝術	yìshù	N	art	29
意见	意見	yìjiàn	N	idea, suggestion	29
意思	意思	yìsi	N	meaning	29
隐私	隱私	yǐnsī	N	privacy	32
迎客松	迎客松	Yíngkèsōng	PN	Welcoming Pine (on Mt. Huang)	31
由	由	yóu	Prep	(to be done) by (sb.)	37
游	游	yóu	V	to travel, to tour	31
游船	游船	yóuchuán	N	pleasure boat	34
游览	游覽	yóulǎn	V	to go sight-seeing, to tour	32

友好	友好	yǒuhǎo	A	friendly	32
友谊	友誼	yǒuyì	N	friendship	28
有时	有時	yǒushí	Adv	sometimes	36
有时候	有時候	yǒushíhou	Adv	sometimes	36
愉快	愉快	yúkuài	A	happy, pleasant	37
羽绒服	羽絨服	yǔróngfú	N	down coat	36
玉兰	玉蘭	Yùlán	PN	Yulan (name of a Chinese girl)	38
园艺	園藝	yuányì	N	gardening	29
园艺师	園藝師	yuányìshī	N	horticulturist	29
约	約	yuē	V	to ask or invite (in advance)	37
月饼	月餅	yuèbing	N	moon cake	28
月亮	月亮	yuèliang	N	moon	28
岳父	岳父	yuèfù	N	father-in-law (the wife's father)	38
岳母	岳母	yuèmǔ	N	mother-in-law (the wife's mother)	38
越……越……	越……越……	yuè……yuè……		the more ... the more ...	37
晕	暈	yūn	V	to feel dizzy	34
云	雲	yún	N	cloud	31
晕船	暈船	yùnchuán	VO	to feel sick because of the movement of a boat or ship	34

Z

再说	再説	zàishuō	Conj	what's more	34
藏趣园	藏趣園	Zàngqùyuán	PN	the Tibetan Botanical Garden	33
早上	早上	zǎoshang	N	(early) morning	30
债	債	zhài	N	debt	35

长	長	zhǎng	V	to grow	29
账	賬	zhàng	N	account, bill	37
账单	賬單	zhàngdān	N	bill	37
照相	照相	zhàoxiàng	VO	to take a picture	32
这样	這樣	zhèyàng	Pr	so, such	27
珍贵	珍貴	zhēnguì	A	valuable, precious	36
整齐	整齊	zhěngqí	A	neat, tidy	29
正常	正常	zhèngcháng	A	normal	27
正确	正確	zhèngquè	A	correct	31
政府	政府	zhèngfǔ	N	government	38
挣	挣	zhèng	V	to earn	32
⋯⋯之一	⋯⋯之一	⋯⋯zhī yī		one of	28
知识	知識	zhīshi	N	knowledge	31
植树	植樹	zhíshù	VO	to plant trees	33
植树节	植樹節	Zhíshù Jié	PN	Arbor Day	33
植物	植物	zhíwù	N	plant	33
植物园	植物園	zhíwùyuán	N	botanical garden	33
止	止	zhǐ	V	to stop	34
只是	祇是	zhǐshì	Adv	just, merely	38
只要	祇要	zhǐyào	Conj	as long as	31
指	指	zhǐ	V	to point at	34
中华	中華	Zhōnghuá	PN	China	31
中间	中間	zhōngjiān	N	middle, center	32
中秋节	中秋節	Zhōngqiū Jié	PN	Mid-Autumn Festival	28
重要	重要	zhòngyào	A	important	28
珠穆朗玛峰	珠穆朗瑪峰	Zhūmùlǎng-mǎ Fēng	PN	Mount Qomolangma (known in the West as Mount Everest)	31
主意	主意	zhǔyi	N	idea	33

住房	住房	zhùfáng	N	house, housing	32
壮观	壯觀	zhuàngguān	A	grand, spectacular, magnificent	34
准备	準備	zhǔnbèi	V	to prepare	28
自然	自然	zìrán	N/A	nature; natural	31
*字	字	zì	N	character, handwriting	29
字画	字畫	zìhuà	N	calligraphy and painting	29
嘴	嘴	zuǐ	N	mouth	27
最	最	zuì	Adv	most	27
最好	最好	zuìhǎo	Adv	had better	36
最后	最後	zuìhòu	N	final, last	37
最近	最近	zuìjìn	N	recently	30
尊敬	尊敬	zūnjìng	V	to respect, to honor	37
尊重	尊重	zūnzhòng	V	to respect	28
作品	作品	zuòpǐn	N	work of literature or art	29
做操	做操	zuòcāo	VO	to do gymnastics	30

补充生词
Supplementary Words

词条	繁体	拼音	词性	英译	课号

A

| 矮 | 矮 | ǎi | A | short | 28 |
| 奥林匹克 | 奥林匹克 | Àolínpǐkè | PN | the Olympics | 30 |

B

保健品	保健品	bǎojiànpǐn	N	health care products	27
保姆	保姆	bǎomǔ	N	maid	37
鼻烟壶	鼻煙壺	bíyānhú	N	snuff bottle	34
鼻子	鼻子	bízi	N	nose	29
部门	部門	bùmén	N	department	32

C

参考	参考	cānkǎo	V	to provide reference	29
藏	藏	cáng	V	to hide	38
长寿	長壽	chángshòu	A	longevity	30
嫦娥	嫦娥	Cháng'é	PN	Chang'e (a goddness lived in the Lunar Palace)	28
嫦娥奔月	嫦娥奔月	Cháng'é bèn yuè	IE	Chang'e flew to the moon	28
炒	炒	chǎo	V	to stir-fry	37
词典	詞典	cídiǎn	N	dictionary	37

| 聪明 | 聰明 | cōngming | A | intelligent, clever | 30 |
| 存款 | 存款 | cúnkuǎn | N/VO | bank savings; to deposit money | 35 |

D

打鱼	打魚	dǎ yú	V O	to go fishing	34
大部分	大部分	dà bùfen		majority	35
贷款	貸款	dàikuǎn	VO/N	to provide or ask for a loan; loan	32
导演	導演	dǎoyǎn	N/V	director; to direct (a film, play, etc.)	38
灯	燈	dēng	N	lamp, lantern	38
点	點	diǎn	V	to order	37
电视机	電視機	diànshìjī	N	TV set	29
调查	調查	diàochá	V	to investigate	30
掉	掉	diào	V	to fall	34
动物园	動物園	dòngwùyuán	N	zoo	33
段	段	duàn	M	*a measure word used of a section of something long*	31
对	對	duì	V	to match	38
对联	對聯	duìlián	N	antithetical couplet	38

E

| 阿弥陀佛 | 阿彌陀佛 | Ēmítuófó | N | merciful Buddha, May Buddha preserve us | 27 |
| 耳朵 | 耳朵 | ěrduo | N | ear | 33 |

F

| 飞虎旗 | 飛虎旗 | fēihǔqí | N | a banner with the pattern of a flying tiger on it | 38 |

| 奋斗 | 奮鬥 | fèndòu | V | to struggle, to strive | 35 |

G

改善	改善	gǎishàn	V	to improve	31
高薪	高薪	gāoxīn	N	high salary	35
工程	工程	gōngchéng	N	project	31
工程师	工程師	gōngchéngshī	N	engineer	32
工具	工具	gōngjù	N	tool	32
工艺品	工藝品	gōngyìpǐn	N	handicraft product	34
公里	公里	gōnglǐ	M	kilometer	30
古代	古代	gǔdài	N	ancient times	28
故乡	故鄉	gùxiāng	N	hometown	30
关心	關心	guānxīn	V	to care for	29
官	官	guān	N	government official	36
柜子	櫃子	guìzi	N	cupboard	29
果树	果樹	guǒshù	N	fruit tree	34

H

韩愈	韓愈	Hán Yù	PN	Han Yu (a Chinese litterateur of the Tang Dynasty)	36
杭州	杭州	Hángzhōu	PN	Hangzhou (a city in China)	31
和尚	和尚	héshang	N	Buddhist monk	27
滑	滑	huá	V	to slide	32
华山	華山	Huà Shān	PN	a famous mountain in Shaanxi Province of China	28

画像	畫像	huàxiàng	N	portrait	34
皇宫	皇宫	huánggōng	N	imperial palace	28
汇合	匯合	huìhé	V	to converge	31

J

激烈	激烈	jīliè	A	intense	32
计划	計劃	jìhuà	V	to plan	37
计划生育	計劃生育	jìhuà shēngyù		family planning	37
贾岛	賈島	Jiǎ Dǎo	PN	Jia Dao (a Chinese poet of the Tang Dynasty)	36
健康	健康	jiànkāng	A	healthy	30
江南	江南	Jiāngnán	PN	areas south of the Changjiang River	31
将军	將軍	jiāngjūn	N	general	34
将军服	將軍服	jiāngjūnfú	N	general's uniform	34
交际	交際	jiāojì	V	to communicate	35
轿子	轎子	jiàozi	N	sedan chair	36
今朝有酒今朝醉	今朝有酒今朝醉	jīn zhāo yǒu jiǔ jīn zhāo zuì		"Get drunk while there is still wine"; to indulge oneself for the moment without caring about the future	35
经过	經過	jīngguò	V	to pass, to go by	36
经验	經驗	jīngyàn	N	experience	32
精神	精神	jīngshen	A	spirited	27
竞争	競爭	jìngzhēng	V	to compete	32
敬	敬	jìng	V	to offer politely	27
卷	卷	juǎn	V	to roll up	38
决定	決定	juédìng	V	to decide	33

L

拉	拉	lā	V	to pull	36
老虎	老虎	lǎohǔ	N	tiger	38
老舍	老舍	Lǎo Shě	PN	Lao She (one of the modern Chinese writers)	27
量	量	liáng	V	to measure	28
留	留	liú	V	to stay	33
流传	流傳	liúchuán	V	to spread	30
柳树	柳樹	liǔshù	N	willow	31
乱	亂	luàn	A	at random, at will	35
轮椅	輪椅	lúnyǐ	N	wheelchair	34

M

猫	貓	māo	N	cat	33
毛驴	毛驢	máolú	N	donkey	36
美德	美德	měidé	N	virtue	35
美的	美的	Měidí	PN	a famous brand of electric instrument in China	28
美化	美化	měihuà	V	to beautify	29
秘诀	秘訣	mìjué	N	secret (of success)	30
描写	描寫	miáoxiě	V	to describe	36
墨镜	墨鏡	mòjìng	N	sunglasses	33

N

南水北调	南水北調	nán shuǐ běi diào	IE	to divert water from the south to the north	31

难过	難過	nánguò	A	sad, upset	29
鸟	鳥	niǎo	N	bird	36
鸟宿池边树	鳥宿池邊樹	Niǎo sù chí biān shù		A bird perches on a tree at night by the side of the pool.	36

P ....

胖	胖	pàng	A	fat	33
皮包	皮包	pípāo	N	leather handbag	29
片儿	片兒	piànr	N	slice	27
飘扬	飄揚	piāoyáng	V	to flutter	38
破费	破費	pòfèi	V	to spend money	28

Q ....

奇特	奇特	qítè	A	peculiar, unusual	38
旗子	旗子	qízi	N	flag, banner	38
前途	前途	qiántú	N	future	32
抢救	搶救	qiǎngjiù	V	to save, to rescue	33
巧云	巧雲	Qiǎoyún	PN	Qiaoyun (name of a young maid)	37
庆祝	慶祝	qìngzhù	V	to celebrate	38
穷人	窮人	qióngrén	N	the poor	35

R ....

人间	人間	rénjiān	N	the human world	28
肉丝	肉絲	ròusī	N	shredded meat	37
肉丝炒竹笋	肉絲炒竹笋	ròusī chǎo zhúsǔn		stir-fried shredded pork with bamboo shoots	37

S

僧敲月下门	僧敲月下門	Sēng qiāo yuè xià mén		A monk knocks on a gate under the moon (moonlight).	36
沙发	沙發	shāfā	N	sofa	29
上联	上聯	shànglián	N	first line of a couplet	38
神话	神話	shénhuà	N	fairy tale	28
生育	生育	shēngyù	V	to give birth to	37
诗人	詩人	shīrén	N	poet	31
时装	時裝	shízhuāng	N	fashion	29
使者	使者	shǐzhě	N	envoy	33
收藏	收藏	shōucáng	V	to collect	34
书法家	書法家	shūfǎjiā	N	calligrapher	27
思考	思考	sīkǎo	V	to think deeply	36
寺庙	寺廟	sìmiào	N	temple	27
宋代	宋代	Sòngdài	PN	Song Dynasty	27
苏东坡	蘇東坡	Sū Dōngpō	PN	Su Dongpo (a famous Chinese writer of the Song Dynasty)	27
隋炀帝	隋煬帝	Suí Yángdì	PN	Emperor Suiyangdi (569~618, an emperor of the Sui Dynasty)	31

T

唐朝	唐朝	Tángcháo	PN	Tang Dynasty	28
唐明皇	唐明皇	Táng Mínghuáng	PN	Emperor Tangminghuang (an emperor of the Tang Dynasty)	28
淘汰	淘汰	táotài	V	to eliminate through selection or competition	32

消费	消費	xiāofèi	V	to consume	35
血	血	xiě	N	blood	34
心灵	心靈	xīnlíng	N	soul	29
心脏	心臟	xīnzàng	N	heart	30
醒	醒	xǐng	V	to wake up	28
胸	胸	xiōng	N	chest	27
熊	熊	xióng	N	bear	33
熊猫	熊貓	xióngmāo	N	panda	33
学历	學歷	xuélì	N	record of formal schooling, educational background	32

Y

研究	研究	yánjiū	V	to study, to research	31
眼睛	眼睛	yǎnjing	N	eye	29
扬州	揚州	Yángzhōu	PN	Yangzhou (a city in China)	31
引	引	yǐn	V	to divert, to lead	31
饮料	飲料	yǐnliào	N	drink	27
优	優	yōu	A	excellent	37
优生优育	優生優育	yōushēng yōuyù		bear and rear healthy babies	37
原来	原來	yuánlái	N	formerly, originally	28
缘分	緣分	yuánfèn	N	predestined opportunity for people to be brought together	34
院子	院子	yuànzi	N	courtyard	29
月宫	月宫	yuègōng	N	the Lunar Palace	28
岳父	岳父	yuèfù	N	father-in-law (the wife's father)	
岳母	岳母	yuèmǔ	N	mother-in-law (the wife's mother)	
运动	運動	yùndòng	V/N	to do physical exercise; sports	30

运河	運河	yùnhé	N	canal	31

Z

在于	在于	zàiyú	V	to depend on, to rely on	30
蘸	蘸	zhàn	V	to dip	27
张学良	張學良	Zhāng Xuéliáng	PN	Zhang Xueliang (name of a well-known Chinese general of the 1930s)	34
照顾	照顧	zhàogù	V	to look after	29
珍贵	珍貴	zhēnguì	A	valuable, precious	34
珍稀	珍稀	zhēnxī	A	rare	33
支持	支持	zhīchí	V	to support	32
中国野生动物保护协会	中國野生動物保護協會	Zhōngguó Yěshēng Dòngwù Bǎohù Xiéhuì	PN	China Wildlife Conservation Association	33
中榜	中榜	zhòngbǎng	VO	to become a successful candidate or applicant in the imperial examination	38
竹笋	竹笋	zhúsǔn	N	bamboo shoot	37
竹叶	竹葉	zhú yè		bamboo leaf	33
竹子	竹子	zhúzi	N	bamboo	37
主人	主人	zhǔrén	N	host, master	37
追求	追求	zhuīqiú	V	to pursue	35
走马灯	走馬燈	zǒumǎdēng	N	running horse lantern—lantern with such rotating shadow figures as horses, etc.	38
组	組	zǔ	M	set, series, group	30

汉字索引
Character Index

H

寒	hán	36
汗	hàn	30
河	hé	31
呼	hū	32
胡	hú	38
壶	hú	27
湖	hú	34
互	hù	29
环	huán	33
婚	hūn	32

J

积	jī	31
纪	jì	28
季	jì	36
迹	jì	31
既	jì	33
继	jì	33
绩	jì	31
架	jià	29
嫁	jià	38
艰	jiān	35
俭	jiǎn	35
简	jiǎn	30
剑	jiàn	30
健	jiàn	30
疆	jiāng	37
讲	jiǎng	34
浇	jiāo	29
轿	jiào	38

较	jiào	29
接	jiē	33
街	jiē	30
杰	jié	38
结	jié	32
解	jiě	27
界	jiè	31
金	jīn	35
筋	jīn	38
近	jìn	33
惊	jīng	28
净	jìng	27
敬	jìng	37
静	jìng	27
境	jìng	33
究	jiū	33
居	jū	38
矩	jǔ	38
句	jù	29
决	jué	33
绝	jué	35
君	jūn	29

K

咖	kā	27
靠	kào	33
科	kē	33
棵	kē	31
克	kè	38
筷	kuài	27
困	kùn	35
括	kuò	31

L

辣	là	34
兰	lán	29
篮	lán	31
榄	lǎn	37
朗	lǎng	31
李	lǐ	34
丽	lì	32
俩	liǎ	38
连	lián	34
凉	liáng	34
量	liáng	38
聊	liáo	27
灵	líng	33
令	lìng	33
陆	lù	31
罗	luó	31
锣	luó	30
络	luò	32

M

玛	mǎ	31
蒙	měng	36
迷	mí	34
命	mìng	35
漠	mò	33
穆	mù	31

N

闹	nào	27

《新实用汉语课本》简介
A Brief Introduction to *New Practical Chinese Reader*

刘珣　主编

Editor-in-Chief : Liu Xun

　　《新实用汉语课本》是一套专为海外非华裔成人学习者研制的零起点综合汉语教材。它坚持语言结构为纲，结构与功能、文化相结合的教学理念，力图通过语言结构、语言功能与相关文化知识的学习和听说读写技能训练，逐步培养学习者运用汉语进行交际的能力。教材强调功能项目的教学，内容题材广泛；板块式安排，使核心内容和补充内容分割清晰又易于根据需要进行选择。

　　New Practical Chinese Reader is a set of comprehensive Chinese language textbooks compiled for the purpose of teaching Chinese to adult non-native Chinese speakers without previous Chinese learning experience. The teaching concepts *New Practical Chinese Reader* upholds are taking language structure as the guideline and combining the teaching of language structure with the teachings of language functions and culture. By placing the focus of study on language structure and functional, cultural knowledge, as well as skills training for listening, speaking, reading and writing, *New Practical Chinese Reader* aims to foster learners' ability to communicate in the Chinese language. It emphasizes the instructions of functional items and covers a wide range of topics. The book is divided into units, making it easy for users to differentiate the core content from the supplementary one and choose the content based on their needs.

　　自2002年陆续出版以来，《新实用汉语课本》受到世界各地汉语学习者和汉语教师们的欢迎与关注，总发行量已达百万册，并有版权输出，成为世界上最广泛使用的基础汉语教材之一。已被美国哈佛大学、斯坦福大学、加州大学伯克利分校，加拿大多伦多大学，英国牛津大学、剑桥大学、伦敦大学，德国柏林大学，澳大利亚墨尔本大学，日本早稻田大学等世界著名大学所采用。

　　Since *New Practical Chinese Reader* was published in 2002, it has been well received by learners and teachers of Chinese around the world and aroused a lot of concern among them. With its total circulation hitting 1 million and its copyright imported to other countries, *New Practical Chinese Reader* has become one of the most popular basic Chinese teaching materials that are used by world renowned universities, such as Harvard University, Stanford University and University of California, Berkeley in the United States, Toronto University in Canada, Oxford University, Cambridge University and University of London in Britain, University of Berlin in Germany, University of Melbourne in Australia and Waseda University in Japan.

　　目前已出版了英文注释的简体字版和繁体字版，另有泰文、俄文、西班牙文注释本，以及2009年精心打造的9个语种（英语、法语、德语、俄语、西班牙语、阿拉伯语、日语、韩国语、泰语）的入门级立体化教材（包括图书、CD和多媒体CD-ROM）。

　　Its simplified Chinese character version and traditional Chinese character version with English annotation have been published so far besides its simplified Chinese character version with Thai, Russian and Spanish annotations. The books (with CD and CD-ROM) were also annotated in 9 languages (English, French, German, Russian, Spanish, Arabic, Japanese, Korean, Thai) in 2009 as a set of comprehensive teaching materials for beginners.

《新实用汉语课本》（第2版）（英文注释本1—4册）

New Practical Chinese Reader (2nd Edition)(Annotated in English, Book 1 ~ 4)

　　自2002年陆续出版以来，《新实用汉语课本》受到广大教师和学习者的欢迎，2010年我们推出了第2版。考虑到使用者的方便，教材整体框架未作大的变化，综合了原版在海外使用的课堂实践经验，为读者呈现与时俱进的内容，坚持语言实用，结合实际，培养学习者跨文化交际的能力。

　　第2版繁体字课文放在出版社网站上（www.blcup.com），供使用者免费下载。第2版每一册课本、综合练习册和教师用书都随书附赠1张MP3光盘，录有书中相关听力内容。

　　Since *New Practical Chinese Reader* was published in 2002, it has been well received by teachers and learners of Chinese. Its second edition was published in 2010. For users' convenience, in this new edition we didn't revise the framework, but presented the updated materials in combination with how it was used in foreign countries. The language used is still practical and reality-based so as to foster students' cross-cultural communication skills.

　　Users can visit www.blcup.com and free download the traditional Chinese version of the texts of *New Practical Chinese Reader*'s second edition. In this edition, each Textbook, Workbook and Instructor's Manual comes along with a free MP3 which contains the corresponding listening materials.

课本1（附1张MP3）
ISBN 978-7-5619-2623-9
定价：¥68.00
出版日期：2010年3月

课本2（附1张MP3）
ISBN 978-7-5619-2895-0
定价：¥68.00
出版日期：2010年12月

课本3（附1张MP3）
ISBN 978-7-5619-3255-1
定价：¥70.00
出版日期：2012年3月

课本4（附1张MP3）
ISBN 978-7-5619-3431-9
定价：¥72.00
出版日期：2012年12月

综合练习册1（附1张MP3）
ISBN 978-7-5619-2622-2
定价：¥35.00
出版日期：2010年3月

综合练习册2（附1张MP3）
ISBN 978-7-5619-2893-6
定价：¥38.00
出版日期：2010年11月

综合练习册3（附1张MP3）
ISBN 978-7-5619-3207-0
定价：¥44.00
出版日期：2011年12月

综合练习册4（附1张MP3）
ISBN 978-7-5619-3388-6
定价：¥46.00
出版日期：2012年11月

教师用书1（附1张MP3）
ISBN 978-7-5619-2621-5
定价：¥35.00
出版日期：2010年3月

教师用书2（附1张MP3）
ISBN 978-7-5619-2894-3
定 价：¥32.00
出版日期：2010年11月

教师用书3（附1张MP3）
ISBN 978-7-5619-3303-9
定价：¥35.00
出版日期：2012年6月

教师用书4（附1张MP3）
ISBN 978-7-5619-3387-9
定价：¥35.00
出版日期：2012年10月

《新实用汉语课本》课文情景会话DVD
DVD Version of *New Practical Chinese Reader*

《新实用汉语课本》（英文注释本）1—4册每册配有课文情景会话高清DVD 1张，紧密结合课本，采用真人表演形式，生动再现本课交际场景和会话内容。DVD可随简体版课本购买，也可单独购买。

New Practical Chinese Reader (Annotated in English, Book 1~4) also has the accompanying situational dialogues in a high-definition DVD, which is closely in combination with the texts with authentic vividness. The DVD can be sold with the simplified Chinese version textbook or sold independently.

DVD随书购买　DVD sold together with the book

课本1
（附赠课文情景会话DVD）
ISBN 978-7-5619-1040-5
定价：¥88.00
出版日期：2002年3月

课本2
（附赠课文情景会话DVD）
ISBN 978-7-5619-1129-7
定价：¥98.00
出版日期：2002年11月

课本3
（附赠课文情景会话DVD）
ISBN 978-7-5619-1251-5
定价：¥90.00
出版日期：2003年11月

课本4
（附赠课文情景会话DVD）
ISBN 978-7-5619-1319-2
定价：¥100.00
出版日期：2004年7月

DVD单独购买　DVD sold independently

课文情景会话DVD 1

ISBN 978-7-88703-975-0
定价：¥45.00
出版日期：2010年6月

课文情景会话DVD 2

ISBN 978-7-88703-976-7
定价：¥45.00
出版日期：2010年6月

课文情景会话DVD 3

ISBN 978-7-88703-977-4
定价：¥49.00
出版日期：2010年6月

课文情景会话DVD 4

ISBN 978-7-88703-978-1
定价：¥49.00
出版日期：2010年6月